Updated

BARBADOS

Vacation Guide 2024

Unveiling The Soul of The Caribbean Islands, With Insider Tips, Breathtaking Beaches, Must See Attractions, Top Things To Do, Festivals and Vibrant Culture

Anya Silver

Acknowledgement and Disclaimer

We have dedicated significant effort to ensure that this travel guide provides accurate and up-to-date information as of its publication date. However, we recognize that certain details such as contact information, operating hours, pricing, and travel details may be subject to change. We cannot be held responsible for any inconvenience that may arise from using this guide or for the accuracy and suitability of information sourced from third parties.

We strongly encourage readers to independently verify the information presented in this guide and to confirm any specifics with the relevant establishments or authorities before concluding travel plans. Please stay vigilant for any updates or changes that may occur after the publication of this guide.

Your safety and satisfaction are our top priorities, and we sincerely appreciate your understanding of the dynamic nature of travel-related information. We hope that this guide enhances your journey and serves as a valuable resource throughout your travels.

Table Of Contents

INTRODUCTION: WELCOME TO BARBADOS

Welcome to the "updated Barbados Vacation Guide" your passport to a tropical paradise, where the sun kisses your skin, the turquoise waters beckon, and the rhythm of island life invites you to dance. But before we dive into the heart of Barbados, let me take a moment to greet you with a warm Bajan "Hello!"

This guide is not just any travel book; it's a doorway to adventure, relaxation, and unforgettable moments. We've crafted it with love, passion, and a touch of the sea breeze, ensuring it's as welcoming as the locals themselves.

Why choose Barbados for your next getaway, you ask? Let me share a little story. A while ago, I had the incredible opportunity to visit this enchanting island with my family. Talk about palm-fringed beaches, a vibrant kaleidoscope of coral reefs, and the sweet melodies of calypso music lingering in the air. Our journey was filled with moments of pure bliss, like sipping coconut water straight from the source and watching our kids build sandcastles on some of the world's most pristine beaches.

With each sunset, we fell in love with the island all over again, as the sky transformed into a canvas of fiery oranges and deep purples. As you flip through these pages, I'll sprinkle in a few anecdotes from our own adventures in Barbados, sharing the joy and excitement we experienced.

Barbados isn't just another Caribbean destination; it's a tapestry of cultures, history, and natural beauty. From the vibrant capital of Bridgetown, where colonial history mingles with modern life, to the unspoiled beaches that seem tailor-made for relaxation, this island has something for everyone. You'll explore charming fishing villages, swim with sea turtles in crystal-clear waters, and immerse yourself in the rich heritage of this remarkable place.

But before we set off on this incredible journey, let me share a secret. Barbados isn't just a place; it's an experience. It's the delight of devouring flying fish and cou-cou at a local eatery, the exhilaration of swimming in underground caves, and the exhilaration of dancing to the rhythm of a steel pan band during a festival.

We've packed this guide with amazing things to do and places to see, ensuring you make the most of your Barbadian adventure. Whether you're traveling with family, friends, or embarking on a solo voyage, you'll find something here that resonates with you.

So, dear reader, as you embark on your journey through these pages, envision the warmth of the sun on your skin, the soft caress of the trade winds, and the rhythmic sound of the waves serenading you. Barbados is waiting to capture your heart, leaving you with memories that will last a lifetime.

Getting to Know Barbados

History

Barbados, a jewel in the Caribbean Sea, boasts a history as captivating as its beaches are beautiful. From ancient indigenous settlements to colonial dominance and ultimate independence, this island's story is a tapestry woven with threads of resilience, culture, and transformation.

Long before the arrival of European explorers, the Arawaks and Caribs inhabited Barbados, leaving behind traces of their ancient civilizations. These early inhabitants cultivated a deep connection with the land, fishing its abundant waters and cultivating crops on its fertile soil.

In 1627, Barbados fell under English control, forever changing the course of its history. The British influence left an indelible mark on the island's culture, language, and legal system. Plantations flourished, fueled by the labor of enslaved Africans and indentured servants from

Europe, shaping the island's social and economic landscape.

Barbados became a cornerstone of the British Empire's sugar production, leading to a period of unparalleled prosperity for the island's elite planters. However, this prosperity came at a harrowing human cost, as the brutal system of African slavery took root. The scars of this dark chapter still echo through the island's history and culture.

In 1834, emancipation brought newfound freedom to the enslaved population, marking a pivotal moment in Barbadian history. The legacy of this struggle for freedom and equality resonates in the island's vibrant culture and enduring spirit.

Barbados gained independence from British colonial rule on November 30, 1966, becoming a sovereign nation within the British Commonwealth. This momentous occasion marked the beginning of a new era for the island, one characterized by self-governance and a commitment to forging its own destiny.

Today, Barbados stands as a testament to the strength and resilience of its people. The echoes of its complex history are woven into the fabric of daily life, from the charming colonial architecture of Bridgetown to the rhythms of calypso and reggae that fill the air during festivals.

Visitors to Barbados have the privilege of experiencing this living history firsthand, exploring historic sites, engaging with the local culture, and witnessing the enduring legacy of a nation that has overcome adversity with grace and determination.

As you traverse the shores of this remarkable island, take a moment to reflect on the centuries that have shaped Barbados into the vibrant, welcoming place it is today. The history of Barbados is not confined to textbooks; it lives and breathes in every corner of this enchanting island.

Culture

Barbados, often referred to as the "Gem of the Caribbean," is a melting pot of vibrant cultures and rich traditions. Steeped in a history that spans centuries, this island nation is a captivating blend of influences from Africa, Europe, and the Caribbean itself.

The heartbeat of Bajan culture echoes through its history. From the arrival of the Arawak and Carib indigenous peoples to the legacy of African slaves and the influence of British colonialism, Barbados has evolved into a unique cultural mosaic. The resilient spirit of the Bajan people shines through in their traditions, music, dance, and cuisine.

Music is the soul of Barbados, and its rhythms pulse through every corner of the island. Calypso, reggae, and soca beats set the stage for lively celebrations and festivals. The sound of steel pan drums and the melodic strumming of the banjo resonate with a deep sense of belonging and community.

Get ready to embark on a unique culinary adventure that will tantalize your taste buds like never before. Bajan cuisine is a tantalizing fusion of flavors, reflecting the island's diverse heritage. From the iconic flying fish and cou-cou to hearty servings of pudding and souse, each dish tells a story of ancestral traditions and the love of good food.

Barbados knows how to throw a party! The island's festivals are a riot of color, music, and dance. The Crop Over Festival, a grand celebration of the sugar harvest, transforms the streets into a carnival of masquerade bands and vibrant costumes. From the Oistins Fish Fry to the Holetown Festival, each event is a joyful reflection of Bajan spirit.

The people of Barbados are known for their genuine warmth and hospitality. A friendly "Good morning!" or a welcoming smile from a local is a common sight. This hospitality extends to the island's vibrant markets, where artisans and vendors take pride in sharing their crafts and stories with visitors.

13

Geographical Location

Nestled in the eastern Caribbean Sea, Barbados is a small island nation that exudes natural beauty and cultural richness. Located at approximately 13.1 degrees North latitude and 59.6 degrees West longitude, it sits as the easternmost island in the Lesser Antilles.

Measuring just 34 kilometers (21 miles) long and 23 kilometers (14 miles) wide, Barbados is a compact island with an abundance of diverse landscapes. The west coast is adorned with tranquil, powdery beaches and calm, crystal-clear waters, making it a haven for sun-seekers. In contrast, the rugged east coast is sculpted by the Atlantic Ocean, boasting dramatic cliffs and powerful surf, perfect for adventurous spirits.

Barbados' geological makeup is equally captivating. A coral island, it boasts an extensive coral reef system that encircles the entire coastline, providing a sanctuary for an array of marine life. The island's highest point, Mount Hillaby, stands at a modest 336 meters (1,102 feet), offering panoramic views of the lush interior and the sparkling Caribbean Sea beyond.

This unique geography makes Barbados a treasure trove for nature enthusiasts, beach lovers, and those seeking both relaxation and adventure. Whether you're basking in the sun on the platinum sands of the west coast or exploring the rugged beauty of the east, Barbados' geography ensures that every corner of this island paradise offers a distinct and unforgettable experience.

Climate

Barbados boasts a delightful tropical climate, where sunshine reigns supreme. With average temperatures ranging from 75°F to 85°F (24°C to 29°C) year-round, it's no wonder why this island paradise is a favorite destination. The trade winds that sweep across the island provide a refreshing breeze, making even the warmest days feel comfortable.

The island experiences two distinct seasons. The dry season, from December to May, is characterized by clear skies and minimal rainfall, making it an ideal time for beachgoers and outdoor activities. The wet season, from June to November, brings occasional tropical showers, but don't worry; they're usually short-lived, leaving the landscape lush and vibrant.

Time Zone

Barbados operates on Atlantic Standard Time (AST), which is UTC-4. There's no need to worry about adjusting your watch; you'll find yourself perfectly in sync with the island's relaxed pace. So, leave your worries behind and let the rhythm of Barbados set the pace for your unforgettable adventure.

When To Go

Barbados is a tropical island with a warm climate year-round. However, there are two main seasons to consider when planning your trip: the dry season and the wet season.

Dry Season (December to May)

The dry season is the most popular time to visit Barbados, as the weather is typically sunny and warm with little rainfall. This period marks the peak season, thus anticipate an increase in prices and larger gatherings due to availability of a plethora of activities.

Wet Season (June to November)

The wet season is less popular than the dry season, but it can be a great time to visit Barbados if you're looking for lower prices and fewer crowds. However, keep in mind that you'll need to be prepared for the possibility of rain, especially during the hurricane season (August to October).

Insider Secrets:

• **Crowds:** Barbados is busiest during the winter months (December to February), when many people from North America and Europe escape the cold weather. The island is also busy during the summer months (June to August), when school holidays are in session. If you're looking to avoid the crowds, consider visiting Barbados during the shoulder seasons (March to May and September to November).

● **Budget:** Barbados is a relatively expensive destination, especially during the peak season. However, it is possible to visit Barbados on a budget if you plan ahead and choose your accommodations and activities carefully. Here are a few tips:

● Stay in a guesthouse or Airbnb instead of a hotel.
● Eat at local restaurants instead of tourist traps.
● Take advantage of free activities, such as hiking, swimming, and visiting the beach.
● Purchase a Barbados Welcome Stamp, which gives you access to a variety of discounts on attractions and activities.

Tips for an Amazing Barbados Experience

1. Consider visiting during the dry season (December to May) for optimal beach weather, or the wet season (June to November) for lush landscapes and fewer crowds.

2. Check passport expiration dates and any visa requirements for your nationality.

3. From luxury resorts to cozy guesthouses, Barbados offers a range of accommodations. Secure your spot in advance for the best options.

4. While taxis and rental cars are available, Barbados' public transportation system is reliable and budget-friendly.

5. Bring light, breathable clothing, a wide-brimmed hat, and of course, plenty of sunscreen.

6. While US dollars are widely accepted, it's a good idea to have some local currency (Barbadian Dollars BBD) on hand for smaller purchases.

7. Purchase a Barbados Welcome Stamp, which gives you access to a variety of discounts on attractions and activities.

8. Consider renting a vehicle to discover the island at your preferred speed.

9. Don't miss out on local delicacies like flying fish, cou-cou, and pepperpot stew. Head to Oistins Fish Fry for an authentic taste.

10. Venture into the heart of Barbados with visits to Harrison's Cave, Welchman Hall Gully, and other natural wonders.

11. Strike up a conversation with locals. Their warmth and friendliness will enrich your journey.

12. Coordinate your trip with one of Barbados' vibrant festivals, like the Crop Over Festival or the Holetown Festival.

13. Relax, unwind, and let the easy-going pace of Barbados wash over you. Leave your stress behind and savor each moment.

14. Whether it's snorkeling with sea turtles or trying your hand at windsurfing, Barbados offers a range of water-based activities for every level of adventurer.

15. Don't miss the opportunity to witness Barbados' legendary sunsets. Find a cozy spot on the beach and let the colors paint the sky.

16. Get off the beaten path and explore some of the island's lesser-known attractions, such as the Andromeda Botanic Gardens, the Barbados Wildlife Reserve, and the Mount Hillaby hiking trail.

17. Enjoy the nightlife at one of the island's many bars and clubs.

18. Take a cooking class and learn how to make some of your favorite Barbadian dishes.

19. Go on a rum tasting tour and learn about the island's rich rum-making history.

20. Charter a boat and go snorkeling or diving in the island's coral reefs.

21. Take a surfing lesson and catch some waves at one of Barbados' many surf spots.

22. Visit a local market and buy some fresh produce, souvenirs, and other goods.

What NOT To Do In Barbados

During one of my visits I had to ask a local who has lived there all her life the things that a tourist is not expected to do in Barbados and here are a few things she shared with me:

1. Don't wear camouflage: Camouflage is illegal to wear in Barbados, as it is reserved for the Barbados Defense Force.

2. Don't touch or eat the Manchineel tree: The Manchineel tree is one of the most poisonous trees in the world. Even the sap can cause severe skin irritation.

3. Don't swim on the east coast: The east coast of Barbados is known for its strong currents and rip tides. It is best to swim on the west coast of the island, where the waters are calmer.

4. Don't feed the monkeys: The monkeys at the Barbados Wildlife Reserve are very cute, but it is important not to feed them. Feeding wild animals can make them aggressive and dependent on humans for food.

5. Don't be disrespectful of the culture and traditions: Barbados is a proud and independent nation with a rich culture and history. Kindly show consideration for the customs and traditions of the local community when you visit.

6. Don't bargain with street vendors: It's not customary to bargain in Barbados, and it can be seen as disrespectful.

7. Don't litter: Barbados is a beautiful island, and it's important to keep it that way. Please dispose of your trash properly.

8. Don't haggle with taxi drivers: Taxi drivers in Barbados have set fares, and it's not appropriate to haggle.

Other things I recommend you shouldn't do include:

• **Staying in Your Comfort Zone:** Don't limit yourself to the confines of your accommodation. Venture out and explore local neighborhoods, markets, and eateries for a true taste of Barbados.

• **Neglecting Safety Precautions:** Avoid venturing into unknown areas after dark, and be mindful of your belongings, especially in crowded areas.

• **Neglecting the Unwritten Rules of the Road:** If you decide to rent a car, keep in mind that we drive on the left side of the road. Take extra care at roundabouts and be aware of local traffic customs

• **Missing Out on Culinary Adventures:** Don't limit your palate to familiar dishes. Embrace Bajan cuisine and try local specialties like cou-cou, pudding and souse, and fried flying fish.

• **Neglecting to Connect with Locals:** Strike up conversations with Barbadians. They love sharing their culture, and you might just uncover hidden gems that aren't in the guidebooks.

21 Facts About Barbados

These facts add layers to the rich tapestry of Barbados' history, culture, and natural wonders. They make exploring the island even more intriguing!

1. Barbados is widely believed to be the birthplace of rum. Mount Gay Distilleries, founded in 1703, is one of the oldest rum producers in the world.

2. The first President of the United States, George Washington, visited Barbados in 1751 when he was just 19 years old. It was his only trip outside of what is now the United States.

3. The flying fish holds a significant place as one of the national symbols representing Barbados. These remarkable fish are known for their ability to "fly" over the water's surface for short distances.

4. Barbados is unique in the Caribbean as it is primarily composed of coral limestone rather than volcanic rock.

5. Barbados boasts the third oldest parliament in the entire Commonwealth, which was established in 1639.

6. Barbados is one of the few Caribbean islands where cars drive on the left side of the road, a remnant of its British colonial history.

7. The Hawksbill sea turtle, one of the rarest species of sea turtles in the world, can be found nesting on Barbados' beaches.

8. In the Christ Church Parish cemetery, there's a famous vault known as the Chase Vault. Legend has it that the coffins inside would rearrange themselves, baffling gravekeepers.

9. Barbados is one of the most densely populated countries in the Caribbean, with over 280,000 residents

living on an island that's only 166 square miles (430 square kilometers) in size.

10. The grapefruit grown in Barbados are often much larger than those found in other parts of the world, making them a unique local specialty.

11. The world-famous singer Rihanna, whose full name is Robyn Rihanna Fenty, was born and raised in Barbados.

12. Unlike many other Caribbean islands, Barbados doesn't have any rivers. Instead, the island relies on underground streams and reservoirs for its fresh water supply.

13. Bridgetown, the capital city, boasts one of the deepest natural harbors in the Caribbean, making it a hub for trade and commerce.

14. The rugged coastline at Bathsheba is known for its fascinating rock formations, shaped by centuries of erosion from the powerful Atlantic waves.

15. Bathsheba's Soup Bowl is famous among surfers for its powerful waves. During certain times of the year, a tidal bore phenomenon occurs, creating even bigger waves that surfers flock to ride.

16. Barbados is home to the world's only cricket ground that is also a UNESCO World Heritage Site. Kensington Oval, located in Bridgetown, has hosted many international cricket matches and tournaments.

17. Barbados is a popular filming location for movies and TV shows. Some of the films that have been filmed in Barbados include Pirates of the Caribbean: On Stranger Tides, Transformers: Revenge of the Fallen, and The Rum Diary.

18. Barbados is home to the bearded fig tree, which is the national tree of the island. The bearded fig tree is a large, spreading tree with distinctive aerial roots.

19. Barbados is a relatively young island, geologically speaking. The approximate age is believed to be about 3 million years.

20. Barbados is home to the Mount Hillaby Hiking Trail, which is the highest point on the island and offers stunning views of the surrounding countryside.

21. Barbados is home to the world's largest collection of Concorde aircraft. The Barbados Concorde Experience is located at Grantley Adams International Airport and features two Concorde aircraft that visitors can explore.

Entry Requirements

You're on the right track to experiencing the sun-soaked beaches, vibrant culture, and warm hospitality of this Caribbean gem. To ensure a smooth journey, it's important to understand the visa and entry requirements. Here's everything you need to know:

1. Visa Exemptions: Barbados has a range of visa exemptions in place for travelers from various countries for stays of up to 6 months. Most notably, citizens of the United States, Canada, the United Kingdom, and European Union member states do not require a visa for short stays.

2. Passport Validity: Ensure that your passport is valid for at least six months beyond your planned departure date from Barbados. This is a common necessity for the majority of international trips.

In addition to a valid passport, all visitors to Barbados must have:

- A return ticket or onward travel ticket
- Proof of sufficient funds to support their stay
- Proof of accommodation for the duration of their stay

3. Visa Application Process: For those who do require a visa, the application process is relatively straightforward. You can apply through the Barbados Visa Application Center in your country or online through the official Barbados Immigration Department website.

4. Types of Visas: Barbados offers various types of visas, including tourist visas, business visas, and student visas. Select the suitable category in accordance with the intent of your visit.

Visitors who are planning to work or study in Barbados must obtain a work permit or student visa. Work permits and student visas can be obtained from the Barbados Immigration Department.

5. Length of Stay: Tourist visas typically allow for stays of up to 90 days, with the possibility of extensions. Be sure to confirm the specific terms of your visa upon approval.

Visitors who are staying in Barbados for more than 6 months must apply for an extension of stay. Applications for extensions of stay can be made at the Barbados Immigration Department.

6. Visa Fees: While there are fees associated with visa applications, they vary depending on your nationality and the type of visa you're applying for. Check the official Barbados Immigration Department website for up-to-date fee information.

7. Visa Processing Time: Visa processing times may vary, so it's advisable to apply well in advance of your planned travel dates. Certain visas can undergo a speedy processing period, whereas others may necessitate several weeks for completion.

8. Immigration and Customs Procedures: Upon arrival in Barbados, you'll go through immigration and customs checks. Have all required documents readily available, including your passport, visa (if applicable), and a return or onward ticket.

9. Yellow Fever Vaccination (if applicable): If you're arriving from a country with a risk of yellow fever transmission, you may need to provide proof of vaccination. Check the World Health Organization's guidelines for specific requirements.

10. Prohibited items: When entering Barbados, certain items are strictly prohibited. These include firearms and ammunition, dangerous weapons, explosives, narcotics and psychotropic drugs, pornographic material, counterfeit goods, articles that violate trademarks or copyrights, fresh fruits and vegetables (unless grown in specific areas and with the required permission; contact the Ministry of Agriculture and Consumer Affairs for further guidance), and articles made of camouflage material.

If you are found attempting to import any of these restricted items into Barbados, they will be confiscated, and you may potentially face legal repercussions.

It's crucial to be aware that the Barbados Customs and Excise Department might have additional restrictions on the importation of specific goods. Therefore, it is highly advisable to consult with the department before your trip to Barbados to ensure that you are not inadvertently carrying any prohibited items.

Remember, visa and entry requirements are subject to change, so it's crucial to check for updates before your trip. By ensuring you have all the necessary documentation and adhering to entry guidelines, you'll set the stage for a seamless and unforgettable Barbadian adventure.

Packing Essentials

Comprehensive Packing Checklist for Your Barbados Vacation, ensuring You Have Everything You Need for a Tropical Escape

Essentials:

1. Passport (Ensure a minimum of six months of remaining validity.)

2. Visa (if required)

3. Travel insurance documents

4. Flight tickets or electronic confirmation

5. Hotel reservation details

6. Emergency contact information

Clothing:

7. Lightweight, breathable clothing (shorts, t-shirts, dresses)

8. Swimwear (bikinis, trunks)

9. Sun hats and sunglasses

10. Light jacket or sweater for cooler evenings

11. Comfortable walking shoes or sandals

12. Flip-flops or beach shoes

13. Underwear and socks

14. Sleepwear

Beach and Pool Essentials:

15. Beach towels (quick-drying)

16. Beach bag or tote

17. Sunscreen (SPF 30 or higher)

18. Sunscreen lip balm

19. Beach umbrella or sunshade

20. Water shoes (for rocky beaches)

21. Snorkeling gear (if you have your own)

22. Inflatable float or water toys

Toiletries:

23. Toiletry bag

24. Shampoo and conditioner (travel-sized)

25. Body wash or soap

26. Toothbrush and toothpaste

27. Hairbrush or comb

28. Razor and shaving cream

29. Deodorant

30. Feminine hygiene products (if needed)

31. Face wash and moisturizer

32. Makeup and cosmetics (if desired)

33. Contact lenses and solution (if applicable)

Health and Medications:

34. Prescription medications (with copies of prescriptions)

35. Over-the-counter medications (pain relievers, allergy meds, etc.)

36. First-aid kit (band-aids, antiseptic, tweezers, etc.)

Electronics and Accessories:

37. Mobile phone and charger

38. Power bank or portable charger

39. Camera, batteries, and charger

40. Adapters and converters (if needed)

41. Headphones or earbuds

42. Travel-sized umbrella (for rain or shade)

Travel Gear:

43. Backpack or day bag for excursions

44. Money belt or neck pouch for valuables

45. Lightweight, foldable travel duffel (for souvenirs)

46. Luggage locks and tags

47. Reusable water bottle

Documents and Necessities:

48. Copy of passport and visa (if required)

49. Travel wallet or pouch for documents and cash

50. Credit/debit cards and some local currency (Barbados Dollars)

Entertainment and Reading Material:

51. Books or e-reader for leisure reading

52. Playing cards or travel games

53. Notebook and pen

Optional Items:

54. Snorkeling guidebook or fish identification cards

55. Binoculars for birdwatching or scenic views

56. Travel guidebook for Barbados

57. Travel-sized sewing kit or safety pins

58. Laundry bag or disposable laundry sheets

Remember to adapt this checklist based on your personal preferences and specific needs. Pack smart, and leave some space for souvenirs and treasures you might pick up along the way.

Getting to Barbados

From the UK

There are direct flights to Barbados from several major UK airports, including London Heathrow, London Gatwick, and Manchester. The duration of the flight is approximately eight hours and thirty minutes.

If you're flying from a regional UK airport, you may need to connect through a major hub like London, Miami, or New York before reaching Barbados.

From the USA

There are direct flights to Barbados from several major US airports, including New York JFK, Miami International, and Atlanta Hartsfield-Jackson. The duration of the flight is roughly 4 hours and 30 minutes.

If you're flying from a smaller city or a non-hub airport, you may have a layover in one of the major U.S. cities mentioned above.

From Europe

There are direct flights to Barbados from several major European airports, including London Heathrow, Frankfurt Airport, and Paris Charles de Gaulle Airport. The flight time is approximately 8-10 hours, depending on your departure airport.

From Asia

There are no direct flights to Barbados from most Asian airports. However, you can connect to a flight to Barbados from a major hub airport, such as Dubai International Airport or Singapore Changi Airport. The total travel time will vary depending on your departure airport and connection time.

From Canada

There are direct flights to Barbados from Toronto Pearson International Airport and Montreal-Pierre Elliott Trudeau International Airport. The flight time is approximately 4-5 hours, depending on your departure airport.

If you're departing from a smaller Canadian city, you may have a layover in a major hub like Toronto or Montreal before continuing to Barbados.

Once you arrive at Grantley Adams International Airport in Barbados, you can take a taxi, bus, or rental car to your final destination.

Here are some additional tips for getting to Barbados:

● Book your flights in advance, especially if you are traveling during peak season.
● Compare prices from different airlines and travel websites to get the best deal. Websites and apps like Google Flights, Skyscanner, and Kayak can help you compare prices across multiple airlines and booking platforms.
● Pack light so that you can avoid baggage fees.
● Be prepared for the possibility of delays and cancellations.

• Whenever feasible, consider maintaining flexibility in your travel dates. This can help you find better deals.

• While direct flights are convenient, connecting flights can sometimes be more cost-effective.

• Keep an eye out for airline promotions or special deals that may offer discounted fares to Barbados.

Other additional information

• You can take a ferry from Miami, Florida to St. Thomas, US Virgin Islands. The ferry ride takes approximately 4 hours. From St. Thomas, you can take a connecting ferry to Barbados. The ferry journey between St. Thomas and Barbados typically spans around three hours in duration.

• You can take a ferry from Fort Lauderdale, Florida to Freeport, Bahamas. The ferry ride takes approximately 3.5 hours. From Freeport, you can take a connecting ferry to Barbados. The voyage from Freeport to Barbados typically lasts around 12 hours by ferry.

• It is important to note that ferry schedules can vary, so it is always best to check with the ferry company in advance of your trip.

• There are 4 countries close to Barbados that can be accessed through ferry from Barbados:

1. Saint Lucia: There is a daily ferry service from Barbados to Saint Lucia. The ferry ride takes approximately 90 minutes. Making it a suitable option for a day trip from Barbados.

2. Saint Vincent and the Grenadines: There is a weekly ferry service from Barbados to Saint Vincent and the Grenadines. The duration of the ferry journey from Barbados is approximately three hours.

3. Grenada: There is a weekly ferry service from Barbados to Grenada. The duration of the ferry journey from Barbados is approximately four hours, fifty minutes.

4. Martinique: There is a weekly ferry service from Barbados to Martinique. The duration of the ferry journey from Barbados is approximately five hours.

- Additionally, there are a number of smaller islands in the Caribbean that can be reached by ferry from Barbados, such as Bequia, Canouan, and Mayreau.

CHAPTER ONE: PLACES TO VISIT IN BARBADOS

Welcome to the heart of your Barbadian adventure! In this chapter, we'll be your guide to the myriad of captivating destinations that await you in this Caribbean jewel. From historic landmarks to natural wonders, Barbados is a tapestry of experiences waiting to be woven into your travel story.

Each location has its own unique charm and story to tell, offering a glimpse into the rich culture and breathtaking beauty that defines this island paradise.

Exploring Bridgetown, the Capital

Welcome to Bridgetown, the vibrant capital of Barbados, where the past gracefully intertwines with the present. This bustling city, with its cobblestone streets and colonial architecture, invites you to walk in the footsteps of history

1. A Historic Gem: Bridgetown, the capital of Barbados, is a historic gem with a rich culture and heritage. The city is home to a number of well-preserved colonial buildings, as well as a vibrant waterfront area with shops, restaurants, and bars.

2. Careenage Waterfront: The Careenage Waterfront is a great place to start your exploration of Bridgetown. Take a stroll along the quays and admire the colorful buildings and boats. Be sure to stop at one of the many restaurants or bars for a drink or a bite to eat.

3. Independence Square: Independence Square is the heart of Bridgetown and a must-see for any visitor. The square is home to a number of important historical landmarks, including the Nelson Statue, the Parliament Buildings, and the St. Mary's Church. Independence Square is a living testament to Barbados' journey to independence. This historic site is where the British flag was lowered for the last time, and the Barbadian flag proudly raised, marking a pivotal moment in the nation's history.

4. Parliament Buildings: The Parliament Buildings are one of the most iconic landmarks in Bridgetown. The buildings were built in the early 17th century and are a fine example of Neo-Gothic architecture. Visitors can take a guided tour of the Parliament Buildings or simply admire the exterior from the outside.

5. Shopping in Bridgetown: Bridgetown is a great place to shop for souvenirs. There are a number of shops in the city that sell traditional Barbadian crafts, as well as international brands. Be sure to check out the Pelican Craft Village and the Bridgetown Market for a wide selection of souvenirs.

Towns and Villages

Beyond the sun-drenched beaches and lush landscapes, lies the heart and soul of Barbados - its towns and villages. Each one, with its own distinct personality and cultural tapestry, invites you to step off the beaten path and immerse yourself in the daily life of this vibrant island.

Speightstown

Speightstown, located on the northwest coast of Barbados, is a charming and historic town known for its colonial architecture and vibrant local culture. It boasts picturesque streets, quaint shops, and a lively atmosphere. Distance from the capital is 12 miles north.

Things to do:

1. Visit the Arlington House Museum, a beautifully preserved 17th-century plantation house.

2. Take a walk along the Speightstown Mural Trail, which features a collection of murals painted by local artists.

3. Visit the Speightstown Fish Market to see fresh fish being brought in and sold.

4. Enjoy a meal at one of the many restaurants in Speightstown, such as The Orange Street Grocer or Fisherman's Pub.

5. Snorkeling and swimming at nearby beaches and exploring historic sites like St. Peter's Parish Church.

Accommodation you can find here include: The Sandy Lane Hotel, The Coral Reef Club and The Fairmont Royal Pavilion.

Other necessary information for tourists:
- Speightstown is a popular destination for cruise ships, so it can get busy on days when ships are in port.
- The town is known for its friendly people and relaxed atmosphere.
- There are a number of beaches located near Speightstown, such as Heywoods Beach and Sandy Lane Beach.

Oistins

Oistins is a lively fishing village on the south coast of Barbados, known for its vibrant nightlife and delicious seafood. It's a frequently visited location by both residents and tourists. Approximately 6 miles (10 km) east of Bridgetown.

Things to do:

1. Visit the Oistins Fish Fry on Friday nights for a lively atmosphere with live music, food stalls, and vendors selling souvenirs.

2. Take a walk along the Oistins Fishing Pier and watch the fishermen bring in their catch.

3. Visit the Barbados Wildlife Reserve to see monkeys, turtles, and other native animals.

4. Enjoy a meal at one of the many restaurants in Oistins, such as Uncle George's Fish Market or Pat's Place.

Accommodation you can find here include: The Crane Resort, The Crystal Cove Hotel and The Bougainvillea Beach Resort.

Other necessary information for tourists:

• Oistins is a popular tourist destination, so it can get busy on weekends and holidays.

• The town is known for its fresh seafood and friendly people.

• There are a number of beaches located near Oistins, such as Accra Beach and Carlisle Bay.

Holetown

Holetown, on the west coast of Barbados, is a historic town that holds a special place in the island's history as the site of the first English settlement in Barbados. It's now a bustling hub with upscale shopping, dining, and cultural attractions. Distance from the capital is about 10 miles west.

Things to do:

1. Visit the Holetown Monument, which marks the site of the first English settlement in Barbados.

2. Take a walk along the Holetown Boardwalk and admire the views of the Caribbean Sea.

3. Visit the Holetown Chattel Village to shop for souvenirs and handicrafts.

4. Enjoy a meal at one of the many restaurants in Holetown, such as The Tides Restaurant or The Beach House Restaurant.

5. Water sports and beach activities along the stunning west coast beaches and visit the historic St. James Parish Church.

Accommodation you can find here include: The Royal Westmoreland Golf Club, The Sandpiper Hotel and The Colony Club Hotel.

Other necessary information for tourists:
• Holetown is a popular destination for weddings and honeymoons.

- The town is known for its upscale shops and restaurants.
- There are a number of beaches located near Holetown, such as Sandy Lane Beach and Mullins Beach.

Bathsheba

Bathsheba, on the rugged east coast of Barbados, is a haven for surfers and nature enthusiasts. Known for its dramatic coastline and unique rock formations, it offers a more tranquil and off-the-beaten-path experience. Distance from the capital is 15 miles east.

Things to do:

1. Visit Bathsheba Beach, a beautiful beach known for its large boulders and dramatic waves.

2. Take a hike in the Andromeda Botanic Gardens, a collection of tropical plants and flowers.

3. Visit the East Coast Surfing Championship in December to see some of the world's best surfers compete.

4. Enjoy a meal at one of the many restaurants in Bathsheba, such as The Sea Egg Restaurant or The Round House Restaurant.

Accommodation that can be found here include: The Atlantis Hotel, The Seaview Hotel and The Coconut Court Beach Hotel.

Other necessary information for tourists:
- Bathsheba is a popular destination for surfers and nature lovers.
- The town is known for its rugged coastline and laid-back atmosphere.
- There are a number of other beaches located near Bathsheba, such as Soup Bowl and Cattlewash Beach.

St. Nicholas

St. Nicholas, nestled on the northern coast of Barbados, is a quiet and scenic village known for its picturesque views of the Atlantic Ocean. It's a place to escape the hustle and bustle and immerse in natural beauty. Distance from the capital is 10 miles east

Things to do:

1. Visit the Barbados Concorde Experience to see two Concorde aircraft up close and learn about the history of supersonic flight.

2. Take a walk along the Grantley Adams Boardwalk and enjoy the views of the Caribbean Sea.

3. Visit the Garrison Historic Area, a UNESCO World Heritage Site that features a number of historic buildings and fortifications.

4. Enjoy a meal at one of the many restaurants in St. Nicholas, such as The Waterfront Restaurant or The Fish Pot Restaurant.

Accommodation that can be found here include: The Hilton Barbados Resort, The Courtyard by Marriott Barbados Bridgetown and The Accra Beach Hotel & Spa.

Other necessary information for tourists:
• St. Nicholas Abbey is a beautifully preserved Jacobean mansion with a history dating back to the 17th century. You can tour around it and the its rum distillery

Cherry Tree Hill

Cherry Tree Hill is a picturesque spot located in the parish of Saint Andrew, known for its stunning views of the east coast of Barbados. This destination is a highly recommended spot for those who appreciate the beauty of nature and have a passion for photography. Distance from the capital is 8 miles east.

Things to do:
1. Visit Cherry Tree Hill to enjoy stunning views of the east coast of Barbados.

2. Visit St. Nicholas Abbey, a historic plantation house that offers tours and rum tastings.

3. Take a walk through the St. Nicholas Abbey Heritage Railway, a scenic railway that runs through the plantation.

4. Enjoy a meal at one of the many restaurants on Cherry Tree Hill, such as The Top Deck Restaurant or The Village Bar and Restaurant.

Accommodation you can find here include: The Sugar Cane Club Hotel, The Sandy Lane Hotel and The Royal Westmoreland Golf Club.

Other necessary information for tourists:
• Cherry Tree Hill is a popular tourist destination, so it can get crowded on weekends and holidays.
• The area is known for its lush scenery and beautiful views.

- There are a number of other beaches located near Cherry Tree Hill, such as Morgan Lewis Beach and Foul Bay Beach.

North Point

North Point, located at the northernmost tip of Barbados, is a rugged and awe-inspiring natural wonder. It's known for its dramatic cliffs, crashing waves, and the iconic Animal Flower Cave. Distance from the capital is 20 miles north.

Things to do:

1. Visit Animal Flower Cave, a sea cave with natural pools and a variety of marine life, including sea anemones and fish.

2. Take a walk along the North Point Trail, a scenic trail that offers views of the coastline and the Atlantic Ocean.

3. Visit the Andromeda Botanic Gardens, a collection of tropical plants and flowers.

4. Enjoy a meal at one of the many restaurants in North Point, such as The Fish Pot Restaurant or The Fisherman's Wharf Restaurant.

Accommodation you can find here include: The Atlantis Hotel, The Seaview Hotel and The Coconut Court Beach Hotel.

Other necessary information for tourists:
- North Point is a popular destination for nature lovers and hikers.
- The area is known for its rugged coastline and dramatic cliffs.
- There are a number of other beaches located near North Point, such as Animal Flower Cave Beach and Sandy Lane Beach.

Soup Bowl

Soup Bowl, nestled within the village of Bathsheba, is renowned internationally as one of the premier surfing spots in the Caribbean. Its powerful waves and stunning backdrop make it a mecca for surf enthusiasts. Distance from the capital is 15 miles east.

Things to do:

1. Go surfing at Soup Bowl, a world-famous surfing spot known for its challenging waves.

2. Take a walk along the Bathsheba Beach, a beautiful beach with large boulders and dramatic waves.

3. Visit the Andromeda Botanic Gardens, a collection of tropical plants and flowers.

4. Enjoy a meal at one of the many restaurants in Bathsheba, such as The Sea Egg Restaurant or The Round House Restaurant.

Accommodation you can find here include: The Atlantis Hotel, The Seaview Hotel and The Coconut Court Beach Hotel.

Other necessary information for tourists:

• Soup Bowl is a popular destination for surfers and experienced swimmers.

• The area is known for its strong currents and rip tides, so it is important to be careful when swimming or surfing.

• There are a number of other beaches located near Soup Bowl, such as Bathsheba Beach and Cattlewash Beach.

Barbados Beaches

Barbados, a Caribbean paradise, is renowned for its pristine beaches that stretch along the coast like golden ribbons. Each beach has its own personality, offering a diverse range of experiences, from vibrant and bustling shores to secluded, tranquil coves.

1. **Accra Beach:** This is one of the most popular beaches in Barbados, and for good reason. The beach boasts a stunning landscape characterized by its velvety, pure-white sand and pristine, transparent waters. The beach is also well-protected from the wind, making it a

great place to relax and soak up the sun. Accra Beach is located on the west coast of Barbados, about 2 miles south of Bridgetown.

Accra Beach offers a variety of activities for visitors to enjoy, including swimming, sunbathing, snorkeling, and jet skiing. There are also a number of restaurants and bars located nearby, so you can easily grab a bite to eat or a drink without having to leave the beach.

Accra Beach has a number of amenities, including restrooms, changing facilities, and showers. There are also a number of beach chairs and umbrellas available for rent.

Accra Beach is a public beach, so it is free to visit. The beach is also open 24 hours a day, so you can visit at any time.

2. **Crane Beach:** Crane Beach is another popular beach in Barbados, and it is known for its natural beauty. The beach is located in a secluded cove, and it is surrounded

by lush greenery and dramatic cliffs. The beach also has pink-tinged sand and clear turquoise water. Crane Beach is located on the east coast of Barbados, about 10 miles south of Bridgetown.

Crane Beach offers a variety of activities for visitors to enjoy, including swimming, sunbathing, and snorkeling. There is also a water sports center located on the beach where you can rent kayaks, paddleboards, and other equipment.

Crane Beach has a number of amenities, including restrooms, changing facilities, and showers. You can find a restaurant and bar situated right by the shoreline as well.

Crane Beach is a public beach, so it is free to visit. However, there is a parking fee for visitors who are not staying at the Crane Resort.

3. **Bottom Bay:** Bottom Bay is a secluded beach located on the south coast of Barbados. The coastline is

enveloped by striking cliffs and abundant greenery, creating a picturesque scene at the beach. The beach also has soft, white sand and clear turquoise water. Bottom Bay is located on the south coast of Barbados, about 15 miles east of Bridgetown.

Bottom Bay is a great place to relax and enjoy the natural beauty of Barbados. The beach is a well-visited destination for activities such as swimming, basking in the sun, and engaging in snorkeling.

Bottom Bay has a few basic amenities, such as restrooms and changing facilities. However, there are no restaurants or bars located on the beach.

Bottom Bay is a public beach, so it is free to visit. However, the beach is only accessible via a steep staircase.

4. **Surfing Spots:** Barbados is a great place to surf, and there are a number of different surf spots located around

the island. Some of the most popular surf spots in Barbados include:

- **Soup Bowl:** Soup Bowl is a world-famous surf spot known for its challenging waves. The spot is located on the east coast of Barbados, about 15 miles east of Bridgetown.
- **Freights Bay:** Freights Bay is another popular surf spot located on the east coast of Barbados. The spot is known for its consistent waves and friendly atmosphere.
- **Surfers Point:** Surfers Point is a surf spot located on the south coast of Barbados. The location is renowned for its strong waves and demanding environmental circumstances.

When surfing in Barbados, it is important to be aware of the strong currents and rip tides. It is also important to wear sunscreen and a hat, and to stay hydrated.

Here are some renowned surfing companies in Barbados along with their contact details:

1. Barbados Surf Trips

- Website: www.barbadossurftrips.com
- Email: info@barbadossurftrips.com
- Phone: +1 246-832-0637

2. Ride The Tide Surf School

- Website: www.ridethetidebarbados.com
- Email: info@ridethetidebarbados.com
- Phone: +1 246-230-7673

3. Zed's Surfing Adventures

- Website: www.zedssurftravel.com
- Email: info@zedssurftravel.com

- Phone: +1 246-233-5051

4. Dread or Dead Surf Shop

- Website: www.dreadordead.com
- Email: dreadordeadsurf@gmail.com
- Phone: +1 246-823-7873

5. Ride The Wave Barbados

- Website: www.ridethewavebarbados.com
- Email: ridethewavebarbados@gmail.com
- Phone: +1 246-256-1522

Remember to contact the surf schools directly for the most up-to-date information on lessons, availability, and any special arrangements they may offer. Enjoy catching waves in Barbados!

5. Carlisle Bay: Carlisle Bay is a beautiful crescent-shaped beach with calm turquoise waters and white sand. It is a popular destination for swimming, sunbathing, snorkeling, and diving. It is located in the west coast of Barbados, near Bridgetown

The beach is also a popular place for swimming, sunbathing, snorkeling, diving, jet skiing, parasailing, stand-up paddleboarding, kayaking and glass-bottom boat tours.

The beach has few basic amenities such as restaurants, Bars, beach chairs and umbrellas for rent, water sports rentals and public restrooms and showers.

Carlisle Bay is a popular tourist destination, so it can get busy, especially on weekends and holidays. There are a number of hotels and resorts located near Carlisle Bay, including the Hilton Barbados Resort and the Accra Beach Hotel & Spa. The beach is also home to the Barbados Turtle Project, a conservation organization that protects sea turtles.

6. Mullins Beach: Mullins Beach is a beautiful beach with calm, clear waters and soft white sand. It serves as a favored spot for indulging in swimming, basking in the sun, and exploring the underwater world through snorkeling. It is located in the west coast of Barbados, between Holetown and Speightstown

Other activities you can do there include jet skiing, parasailing, stand-up paddleboarding, kayaking and glass-bottom boat tours.

It has basic amenities such as restaurants, bars, beach chairs and umbrellas for rent, water sports rentals and public restrooms and showers.

Mullins Beach is a popular tourist destination, but it is generally less crowded than Carlisle Bay. There are a number of hotels and resorts located near Mullins Beach, including The Sandpiper Hotel and The Colony Club Hotel. The beach is also home to the Mullins Bay Beach Bar, a popular spot for lunch, drinks, and live music.

7. **Paynes Bay:** Paynes Bay is a beautiful beach with calm, clear waters and soft white sand. It is a popular destination for swimming, sunbathing, snorkelling, and diving. It is located in the west coast of Barbados, between Holetown and St. James

Other fun activities you can do here include jet skiing, parasailing, stand-up paddleboarding, kayaking and glass-bottom boat tours.

It also has some basic amenities such as restaurants, bars, beach chairs and umbrellas for rent, watersports rentals and public restrooms and showers.

Paynes Bay is a popular tourist destination, but it is generally less crowded than Carlisle Bay. There are a number of hotels and resorts located near Paynes Bay, including the Sandy Lane Hotel and the Fairmont Royal Pavilion. The beach is also home to the Lone Star Restaurant, a popular spot for fine dining.

8. Sandy Lane Beach: Sandy Lane Beach is a beautiful beach with calm, clear waters and soft white sand. It is a popular destination for swimming, sunbathing, snorkeling, and diving. It is located in the west coast of Barbados, near St. James

Other fun activities you can enjoy here include jet skiing, parasailing, stand-up paddleboarding, kayaking, and glass-bottom boat tours

It also has basic amenities such as restaurants, bars, beach chairs and umbrellas for rent, watersports rentals and public restrooms and showers.

Sandy Lane Beach stands as an exceptionally prestigious destination on the shores of Barbados. It is home to the Sandy Lane Hotel, a world-famous luxury resort. The beach is open to the public, but there is a fee to use the beach chairs and umbrellas. Sandy Lane Beach is a popular destination for celebrities and other high-profile visitors.

9. Rockley Beach: Rockley Beach is one of the most popular beaches in Barbados, and it's easy to see why. With its soft, white sand and clear, blue water, it's the perfect place to relax and soak up the sun. There are plenty of amenities available, including sunbeds, umbrellas, and water sports rentals. You can also find a variety of restaurants and bars nearby. Rockley Beach is located on the south coast of Barbados, about 10 miles south of Bridgetown.

Activities include sunbathing, swimming, snorkeling, jet skiing, parasailing, windsurfing, and more.

Amenities include sunbeds, umbrellas, water sports rentals, restaurants, bars, and shops.

Rockley Beach can get crowded, especially on weekends and during peak season. It is essential to remain mindful of the powerful currents and rip tides in the area.

10. Bathsheba Beach: Bathsheba Beach, situated on the eastern coast of Barbados, boasts stunning natural beauty. It's known for its dramatic coastline, with large boulders and crashing waves. Bathsheba Beach is a popular spot for surfing and bodyboarding, but it's also a great place to relax and enjoy the scenery. Bathsheba Beach is located about 15 miles east of Bridgetown.

Activities include surfing, bodyboarding, swimming, sunbathing, and walking.

Amenities include restaurants, bars, and a few shops.

Bathsheba Beach can have strong currents and riptides, so it's important to be careful when swimming. There are also no lifeguards on duty.

11. Soup Bowl: Soup Bowl is a world-famous surfing spot located on the east coast of Barbados. It's known for its challenging waves, which can reach up to 20 feet high. Soup Bowl is not for beginners, but it's a great place to watch experienced surfers from the shore. Soup Bowl is located about 15 miles east of Bridgetown.

Activities include surfing, bodyboarding, and watching the surfers from the shore.

Amenities include restaurants, bars, and a few shops.

Soup Bowl has strong currents and riptides, so it's important to be careful when swimming, even if you're not surfing. There are also no lifeguards on duty.

12. Foul Bay: Foul Bay is a secluded beach located on the north coast of Barbados. It is renowned for its tranquil waters and stunning natural landscapes. Foul Bay is a great place to swim, sunbathe, and snorkel. You can also find a few restaurants and bars nearby. Foul Bay is located about 10 miles north of Bridgetown.

Activities include swimming, sunbathing, snorkeling, and walking.

Amenities include restaurants, bars, and a few shops.

Foul Bay is a popular spot for weddings and other special events, so it's important to check the calendar before you go if you're looking for a secluded beach experience.

Natural Wonders

Barbados, a jewel in the Caribbean, is adorned with an array of natural wonders that captivate the senses. From breathtaking coastal vistas to lush botanical gardens, the island is a canvas painted with nature's finest strokes. In this section, we'll embark on a journey to explore the remarkable landscapes and ecological treasures that define Barbados.

1. Harrison's Cave: Harrison's Cave is a limestone cave system located in the parish of Saint Thomas, Barbados. It is one of the most popular tourist attractions on the island and is known for its stunning crystal formations, waterfalls, and pools. Harrison's Cave is located about 10 miles east of Bridgetown.

How to get there:

- **By car:** Take the ABC Highway east from Bridgetown and follow the signs for Harrison's Cave.

- **By bus:** Take the 27 bus from Bridgetown to Harrison's Cave.

Other necessary information for tourists:

- Cost: Adults, $40 USD, children (5-11 years old), $20 USD

- Contact details: Website: https://chukka.com/destinations/barbados/harrisons-cave / Phone: (246) 416-0800

- Operational hours: Daily from 8:30am to 4:30pm

- Harrison's Cave is a fully guided tour.

- The tour takes about 1.5 hours.

- The cave is well-lit and has paved walkways, so it is suitable for all ages.

- There are restrooms and a gift shop at the cave.

2. **Flower Forest:** Flower Forest is a botanical garden located in the parish of Saint Joseph, Barbados. It is home to a wide variety of tropical plants and flowers,

including orchids, hibiscus, and bougainvillea. Flower Forest is also known for its koi ponds and waterfalls. Flower Forest is located about 15 miles east of Bridgetown.

How to get there:

- **By car:** Take the ABC Highway east from Bridgetown and follow the signs for Flower Forest.
- **By bus:** Take the 27 bus from Bridgetown to Flower Forest.

Other necessary information for tourists:

- Cost: Adults $20 USD, Children (5-11 years old) $10 USD
- Contact details: Website https://www.flowerforestbarbados.com/
- Phone: (246) 433-8144
- Operational hours: Daily from 9:00am to 5:00pm
- Flower Forest is a self-guided tour.
- The tour takes about 1-2 hours.
- The gardens are well-maintained and have paved walkways, so it is suitable for all ages.

- There are restrooms and a gift shop at the gardens.

3. **Animal Flower Cave:** Animal Flower Cave is a sea cave located in the parish of Saint Lucy, Barbados. It is known for its natural pools and a variety of marine life, including sea anemones and fish. Animal Flower Cave is also a popular spot for snorkeling and scuba diving. Animal Flower Cave is located about 10 miles north of Bridgetown.

How to get there:
- By car: Take the ABC Highway north from Bridgetown and follow the signs for Animal Flower Cave.
- By bus: Take the 27 bus from Bridgetown to Animal Flower Cave.

Other necessary information for tourists:
- Cost: Adults $30 USD, Children (5-11 years old) $15 USD
- Contact details: Website: https://www.animalflowercave.com/

Phone: (246) 422-2281

- Operational hours: Daily from 9:00am to 5:00pm
- Animal Flower Cave is a self-guided tour.
- The tour takes about 1 hour.
- The cave is well-lit and has paved walkways, so it is suitable for all ages.
- There are restrooms and a gift shop at the cave.

4. Welchman Hall Gully: Welchman Hall Gully is a tropical ravine located in the central highlands of Barbados. It is home to a variety of plants and animals, including mahogany trees, ferns, orchids, and monkeys. The gully is also home to a waterfall and a number of pools. Welchman Hall Gully can be found in the St. Thomas parish, situated approximately 10 miles to the east of Bridgetown.

You can get to Welchman Hall Gully by car, taxi, or bus. If you are taking the bus, you can take the number 27 bus from Bridgetown to Welchman Hall Gully.

Other necessary information for tourists:

- **Cost:** The entrance fee to Welchman Hall Gully is $20 for adults and $10 for children.

- **Contact details:** The phone number for Welchman Hall Gully is 1 (246) 423-9894.

- **Operational hours:** Welchman Hall Gully is open from 9:00 AM to 5:00 PM, seven days a week.

- Welchman Hall Gully is a relatively easy walk, but there are some steps and uneven surfaces. It is recommended to wear comfortable shoes. There is also a small restaurant and gift shop located at the entrance to the gully.

5. **Barbados Wildlife Reserve:** The Barbados Wildlife Reserve is a sanctuary for indigenous and exotic wildlife nestled in the lush mahogany forests of Barbados. This unique reserve offers visitors the opportunity to observe animals in a natural, open setting, allowing for an up-close and personal encounter with the island's rich biodiversity. Situated in the parish of Saint Peter, the Barbados Wildlife Reserve is easily accessible by car and is approximately a 30-minute drive from

Bridgetown. Follow the signs from major routes, or consider a guided tour for added convenience.

You can get to the Barbados Wildlife Reserve by car, taxi, or bus. If you are taking the bus, you can take the number 27 bus from Bridgetown to the Barbados Wildlife Reserve.

Other necessary information for tourists:

- **Cost:** The entrance fee to the Barbados Wildlife Reserve is $30 for adults and $15 for children.
- **Contact details:** The phone number for the Barbados Wildlife Reserve is 1 (246) 422-3623.
- **Operational hours:** The Barbados Wildlife Reserve is open from 9:00 AM to 5:00 PM, seven days a week.
- The Barbados Wildlife Reserve is a relatively easy walk, but there are some steps and uneven surfaces. It is recommended to wear comfortable shoes. There is also a small restaurant and gift shop located at the entrance to the reserve.

- The reserve also houses a Grenade Hall Forest and Signal Station, offering insights into the island's history and natural heritage.

6. Andromeda Botanic Gardens: Andromeda Botanic Gardens is a botanical garden located in the parish of St. Joseph, about 10 miles east of Bridgetown. The gardens are home to a variety of tropical plants and flowers, including orchids, bromeliads, and ferns. The gardens also have a number of water features, such as streams, waterfalls, and ponds. Andromeda Botanic Gardens is situated in the parish of Saint Joseph, about 10 miles east of Bridgetown.

You can get to Andromeda Botanic Gardens by car, taxi, or bus. If you are taking the bus, you can take the number 27 bus from Bridgetown to Andromeda Botanic Gardens.

Other necessary information for tourists:

- Cost: The entrance fee to Andromeda Botanic Gardens is $20 for adults and $10 for children.

- Contact details: The phone number for Andromeda Botanic Gardens is 1 (246) 433-9330.
- Operational hours: Andromeda Botanic Gardens is open from 9:00 AM to 5:00 PM, seven days a week.
- Other necessary information for tourists: Andromeda Botanic Gardens is a relatively easy walk, but there are some steps and uneven surfaces. It is recommended to wear comfortable shoes. There is also a small restaurant and gift shop located at the entrance to the gardens.

7. **Garrison Savannah:** Garrison Savannah is a large park located in the heart of Bridgetown, Barbados. It is a UNESCO World Heritage Site and is known for its historic significance and natural beauty. The park was once used as a military parade ground, but it is now a popular spot for picnics, concerts, and other events. Garrison Savannah is located at the junction of Broad Street and Constitution River in Bridgetown, Barbados.

The easiest way to get to Garrison Savannah is by taxi or bus. The park is also within walking distance of many hotels and attractions in Bridgetown.

Other necessary information for tourists:

- **Cost:** There is no admission fee to enter Garrison Savannah.

- Contact details: The Garrison Savannah Historic Area is managed by the Barbados National Trust. Their contact information is as follows:

Address: Garrison Historic Area, St. Michael, Barbados

Phone: (246) 426-0944

- Operational hours: Garrison Savannah is open 24 hours a day, 7 days a week.

- Garrison Savannah is a popular spot for locals and tourists alike, so it can be crowded on weekends and during peak season. The park is also home to a number of historical monuments and buildings, so be sure to take some time to explore the area.

8. Codrington College: Codrington College is a theological college located in St. John, Barbados. It is the oldest theological college in the Western Hemisphere and is known for its beautiful grounds and historic buildings. The college is open to the public and visitors can take a guided tour of the grounds and buildings.

Codrington College is located at College Hill, St. John, Barbados. The easiest way to get to Codrington College is by taxi or bus. The college is also within driving distance of Bridgetown.

Other necessary information for tourists:
- **Cost:** There is a small admission fee to enter Codrington College.
- Contact details: Codrington College can be contacted at the following:

Address: College Hill, St. John, Barbados

Phone: (246) 423-0392
- Operational hours: Codrington College is open to the public Monday-Friday, 9:00am-5:00pm.

- Codrington College is a religious institution, so please be respectful of the students and staff. Visitors are also asked to dress appropriately when visiting the college.

8. **Farley Hill National Park:** Farley Hill National Park is a beautiful park located in St. Peter, Barbados. The park is home to the ruins of a 17th-century plantation

house, as well as a variety of tropical plants and flowers. Farley Hill National Park is a great place to relax and enjoy the natural beauty of Barbados. Farley Hill National Park is located at Farley Hill, St. Peter, Barbados.

The easiest way to get to Farley Hill National Park is by taxi or bus. The park is also within driving distance of Bridgetown.

Other necessary information for tourists:

• **Cost:** There is a small admission fee to enter Farley Hill National Park.

• **Contact details:** Farley Hill National Park can be contacted at the following:

Address: Farley Hill, St. Peter, Barbados

Phone: (246) 422-3555

• **Operational hours:** Farley Hill National Park is open to the public Tuesday-Sunday, 8:30am-5:30pm.

• Farley Hill National Park is a popular spot for locals and tourists alike, so it can be crowded on weekends and during peak season. Be sure to wear comfortable shoes and bring sunscreen and water, as there is a lot of walking involved.

Historic Sites and Museums

Barbados, steeped in centuries of history, is a treasure trove of historic sites and museums that narrate its captivating past. From colonial-era architecture to insightful exhibits, each site unveils a chapter of the island's story. In this section, we'll explore the cultural tapestry woven by these landmarks, offering a glimpse into Barbados' vibrant and diverse heritage.

1. **George Washington House:** The George Washington House is a historic house located in Bridgetown, Barbados. It is believed to be the only house outside of the United States where George Washington slept. The house was built in the early 1700s and is now a museum. Located at 135 Roebuck Street, Bridgetown, Barbados.

The George Washington House is located in the heart of Bridgetown, within walking distance of many hotels and attractions. You can also take a bus or taxi to the house.

Other necessary information for tourists:

- **Cost:** Entry to the George Washington House is $10 for adults, $5 for children, and free for children under 5.

- **Activities to do there:** Visitors to the George Washington House can tour the house, learn about its history, and see a variety of exhibits on George Washington and his time in Barbados.

- **Operational hours:** The George Washington House is open from 9:00 AM to 5:00 PM, Monday through Friday.

- Contact details: +1 (246) 426-2729
- The best time to visit the George Washington House is in the morning, when there are fewer crowds.
- There is a small gift shop at the George Washington House where you can buy souvenirs.

- The George Washington House is located in a busy area of Bridgetown, so be careful when crossing the street.

2. **Barbados Museum and Historical Society:** The Barbados Museum and Historical Society is a museum located in Bridgetown, Barbados. It houses a collection of artifacts and exhibits on the history and culture of Barbados. Located at Garrison Savannah, St. Michael, Barbados.

The Barbados Museum and Historical Society is located in the Garrison Savannah, about 1.5 miles south of Bridgetown. The museum is easy to access by car or taxi.

Other necessary information for tourists:

- **Cost:** Entry to the Barbados Museum and Historical Society is $10 for adults, $5 for children, and free for children under 5.

- **Activities to do there:** Visitors to the Barbados Museum and Historical Society can tour the museum, learn about the history and culture of Barbados, and see a variety of exhibits on topics such as slavery, colonialism, and independence.

- **Operational hours:** The Barbados Museum and Historical Society is open from 9:00 AM to 5:00 PM, Monday through Friday.

- Contact details: +1 (246) 427-0919
- The best time to visit the Barbados Museum and Historical Society is in the morning, when there are fewer crowds.
- There is a small gift shop at the Barbados Museum and Historical Society where you can buy souvenirs.
- The Barbados Museum and Historical Society is located in a beautiful area of Bridgetown, so be sure to take some time to walk around and enjoy the scenery.

3. St. Nicholas Abbey: St. Nicholas Abbey is a historic plantation house located in Cherry Tree Hill, Barbados. It is one of the oldest plantation houses in the Caribbean and is still in operation today. Visitors can tour the

91

house, learn about the history of sugar plantations in Barbados, and sample the abbey's rum. Located at Cherry Tree Hill, St. Nicholas, Barbados.

St. Nicholas Abbey is located about 10 miles east of Bridgetown. You can take a bus or taxi to the abbey.

Other necessary information for tourists:
- **Cost:** Entry to St. Nicholas Abbey is $20 for adults, $10 for children, and free for children under 3.

- **Activities to do there:** Visitors to St. Nicholas Abbey can tour the house, learn about the history of sugar plantations in Barbados, sample the abbey's rum, and visit the abbey's distillery.

- **Operational hours:** St. Nicholas Abbey is open from 9:00 AM to 5:00 PM, Monday through Friday.

- **Contact details:** +1 (246) 422-2190
- The best time to visit St. Nicholas Abbey is in the morning, when there are fewer crowds.

- Additionally, there is a souvenir store available where you have the opportunity to buy mementos and keepsakes.
- St. Nicholas Abbey is located in a beautiful area of Barbados, so be sure to take some time to walk around and enjoy the scenery.

4. Morgan Lewis Mill: This is a historic watermill located on the east coast of Barbados. The mill was built in the 17th century and was used to grind sugarcane. Today, the mill is a museum that offers visitors a glimpse into the past of sugar production in Barbados.

Morgan Lewis Mill is located in St. Andrew, Barbados, about 15 miles east of Bridgetown. You can take a taxi or bus to Morgan Lewis Mill from Bridgetown. The bus ride takes about an hour.

Other necessary information for tourists:
- **Cost:** Admission to Morgan Lewis Mill is $20 USD for adults and $10 USD for children.

● **Activities to do there:** Visitors can tour the mill, learn about the history of sugar production in Barbados, and see how the mill operated. Additionally, there is a souvenir store available where you have the opportunity to buy mementos and keepsakes.

● **Operational hours:** Morgan Lewis Mill is open from 9:00am to 5:00pm daily.

● **Contact details:** Telephone: (246) 433-9323

● The best time to visit Morgan Lewis Mill is in the morning or afternoon, when the weather is cooler.

● If you are interested in learning more about the history of sugar production in Barbados, be sure to take the guided tour.

5. **Mount Gay Rum Distillery:** The Mount Gay Rum Distillery is the oldest continuously operating rum distillery in the world. The distillery was founded in 1703 and has been producing rum for over 300 years. Today, the distillery is a popular tourist attraction and offers visitors a tour of the distillery and a tasting of their rum.

The Mount Gay Rum Distillery is located in The Valley, Barbados, about 10 miles east of Bridgetown. You can take a taxi or bus to the Mount Gay Rum Distillery from Bridgetown. The bus ride takes about an hour.

Other necessary information for tourists:
• **Cost:** Admission to the Mount Gay Rum Distillery is $25 USD for adults and $15 USD for children.

• **Activities to do there:** Visitors can take a tour of the distillery, learn about the rum-making process, and sample some of the rum. Additionally, there is a souvenir store available where you have the opportunity to buy mementos and keepsakes.

• **Operational hours:** The Mount Gay Rum Distillery is open from 9:00am to 5:00pm daily.

• **Contact details:** Telephone: (246) 426-0400
• The best time to visit the Mount Gay Rum Distillery is in the morning or afternoon, when the weather is cooler.

- If you are interested in learning more about the history of rum production in Barbados, be sure to take the guided tour.

6. **Sunbury Plantation House:** Sunbury Plantation House is a historic plantation house located on the west coast of Barbados. The house was built in the 18th century and was once one of the most important plantations on the island. Today, the house is a museum that offers visitors a glimpse into the life of a wealthy plantation owner in the 18th century.

Sunbury Plantation House is located in St. Michael, Barbados, about 10 miles west of Bridgetown. You can take a taxi or bus to Sunbury Plantation House from Bridgetown. The bus ride takes about an hour.

Other necessary information for tourists:
- **Cost:** Admission to Sunbury Plantation House is $20 USD for adults and $10 USD for children.

- **Activities to do there:** Visitors can tour the house, learn about the history of plantation life in Barbados, and see the original furniture and furnishings. Additionally, there is a souvenir store available where you have the opportunity to buy mementos and keepsakes.

- **Operational hours:** Sunbury Plantation House is open from 9:00am to 5:00pm daily.

- **Contact details:** Telephone: (246) 422-2195
- The best time to visit Sunbury Plantation House is in the morning or afternoon, when the weather is cooler.
- Wear comfortable shoes, as you will be doing a lot of walking.

7. **Nidhe Israel Synagogue:** Nidhe Israel Synagogue, also known as the Synagogue of the Scattered of Israel, is the oldest synagogue in the Western Hemisphere. It was built in 1654 by Sephardic Jewish settlers who had fled Brazil to escape the Portuguese Inquisition. The synagogue is located in the heart of Bridgetown, Barbados, and is a popular tourist attraction.

Nidhe Israel Synagogue is located on Synagogue Lane, Bridgetown, Barbados. It is bordered by Magazine Lane, James Street, Coleridge Street, and Pinfold Street.

- **By taxi:** Taxis are readily available in Bridgetown. You can ask your taxi driver to take you to Nidhe Israel Synagogue.
- **By bus:** The number 11 bus goes from the Bridgetown bus terminal to Synagogue Lane. Get off at the Synagogue Lane bus stop and walk a short distance to the synagogue.
- **On foot:** If you are staying in Bridgetown, you can walk to Nidhe Israel Synagogue. The distance from the bus terminal is a brief 15-minute stroll away.

The admission fee to Nidhe Israel Synagogue is BDS$25 for adults and BDS$12.50 for children. A special offer is available for groups consisting of 10 or more individuals.

Activities to do there:

1. Tour the synagogue: Visitors can take a guided tour of the synagogue to learn about its history and architecture.

2. Visit the museum: The synagogue complex also includes a museum that houses a collection of Jewish artifacts and exhibits on the history of the Jewish community in Barbados.

3. Attend a service: Visitors are welcome to attend religious services at the synagogue.

4. Shop for souvenirs: There is a gift shop at the synagogue where visitors can purchase souvenirs, such as books, jewelry, and Judaica items.

Nidhe Israel Synagogue is open from Monday to Friday from 9:00 AM to 3:00 PM. The museum also operates on the same days.

Other necessary information for tourists:
- Phone number: (246) 436-6869

- The best time to visit Nidhe Israel Synagogue is during the off-season (May to November), when there are fewer tourists and the weather is more pleasant.
- If you are planning to visit on a Friday, be sure to arrive early to avoid the crowds.
- Be respectful of the religious nature of the site. Dress appropriately and avoid making noise during services.
- There is a small cafe at the synagogue where you can purchase snacks and drinks.
- The synagogue is located in a historic neighborhood, so be sure to take some time to explore the area after your visit.
- Nidhe Israel Synagogue is a wheelchair-accessible site.
- There are restrooms available on site.
- Photography is permitted inside the synagogue, but visitors are asked to be respectful of the religious nature of the site.

Travel Itinerary Planner

_____

_____

_____

_____

_____

_____

_____

_____

_____

_____

_____

_____

CHAPTER TWO: WHAT AND WHERE TO EAT

Barbados, a culinary gem of the Caribbean, invites you on a gastronomic adventure like no other. From mouthwatering seafood to delectable Bajan specialties, the island offers a diverse array of flavors to tantalize your taste buds. In this section, we'll guide you through the best dining spots, from charming local eateries to upscale restaurants, ensuring that every meal in Barbados is a memorable experience.

Barbadian Bajan Cuisine

Barbadian cuisine, often referred to as Bajan cuisine, is a delightful fusion of African, British, Indian, and Caribbean influences. The island's rich culinary heritage is reflected in its diverse range of dishes, each bursting with unique flavors and made from locally-sourced ingredients. Here are some must-try Bajan dishes for an authentic taste of Barbados:

1. Flying Fish and Cou Cou: Flying fish and cou cou is the national dish of Barbados. It consists of fried flying fish served with cou cou, a starchy dish made from cornmeal and okra. Flying fish is a seasonal fish that is caught in the waters around Barbados. It is a delicate fish with a mild flavor. Cou cou is a hearty dish that is often served with a gravy or sauce.

2. Bajan Macaroni Pie: Bajan macaroni pie is a popular comfort food in Barbados. It is made with macaroni noodles, cheese, eggs, and milk. The pie is often flavored with spices such as nutmeg, cinnamon, and cloves. Bajan macaroni pie is typically served as a side dish or as a main course.

3. Bajan Fishcakes: Bajan fish cakes are another popular dish in Barbados. They are made with salted codfish, flour, onions, and spices. The fishcakes are fried until golden brown and crispy. Bajan fishcakes are typically served as a snack or appetizer.

4. Cutters: Cutters are a type of sandwich that is popular in Barbados. They are made with a salt bread roll that is cut in half and filled with meat, fish, or vegetables. Cutters are typically served with a Bajan pepper sauce.

5. Pudding and Souse: Pudding and souse is a traditional Barbadian breakfast dish. It consists of pickled pork (souse) served with sweet potatoes and breadfruit (pudding). Pudding and souse is typically served with a hot sauce.

6. Pepper Pot: Pepper Pot is a hearty stew made with a variety of meats (often pork and beef), cassava, okra, spinach, and a blend of spices like thyme and hot peppers.

7. Conkies: Conkies are sweet treats made from a blend of cornmeal, pumpkin, coconut, and spices, wrapped in a banana leaf and steamed to perfection.
Ingredients: Cornmeal, pumpkin, coconut, raisins, sugar, ginger, nutmeg, butter.

8. Bajan Black Cake: A beloved dessert for special occasions, Bajan Black Cake is a rich and boozy fruitcake made with dried fruits soaked in rum and sherry.

Ingredients: Dried fruits (raisins, currants, prunes), rum, sherry, brown sugar, butter, eggs, flour, nutmeg.

9. Jug Jug: A casserole made with beef and pork mixed together with pigeon peas, onions, corn, thyme, and hot peppers.

10 Beef Stew: Beef Stew is a hearty and comforting dish that showcases tender pieces of beef slow-cooked in a flavorful broth with a medley of vegetables. It's a cherished comfort food in Barbados, perfect for warming the soul.

Ingredients: Beef chunks, onions, garlic, carrots, potatoes, thyme, bay leaves, tomatoes, beef broth, Worcestershire sauce, salt, pepper.

11. Pigtails and Souse: Pigtails and Souse is a unique Bajan delicacy that combines tender, marinated pig tails with a zesty pickled sauce. It's a tangy and savory dish that packs a punch of flavor.

Ingredients: Pig tails, lime or lemon juice, hot peppers, cucumbers, onions, salt, pepper.

12. Pelau: Pelau is a flavorful one-pot dish that brings together tender chicken, pigeon peas, rice, and an array of spices. Cooked in coconut milk, it's a delicious blend of savory and sweet flavors.

Ingredients: Chicken pieces, pigeon peas, rice, coconut milk, pumpkin, carrots, bell peppers, onions, garlic, thyme, brown sugar, soy sauce.

Oistins Fish Fry, A Foodie's Paradise

Oistins, a small fishing village on the south coast of Barbados, is famous for its weekly Fish Fry on Friday nights. This lively event is a must-do for any foodie visiting Barbados.

The Oistins Fish Fry features dozens of stalls selling fresh seafood, cooked to order. You can find everything from grilled mahi mahi to fried flying fish to lobster creole. There are also a number of stalls selling sides such as cou cou, macaroni pie, and coleslaw.

In addition to the food, the Oistins Fish Fry is also a great place to experience Barbadian culture. There is live music, dancing, and shopping. The atmosphere is festive and welcoming, and it's a great place to people-watch.

If you're looking for a delicious and authentic Barbadian dining experience, be sure to check out the Oistins Fish Fry. Here are a few tips for making the most of your visit:

- Arrive early to beat the crowds. The Fish Fry starts at around 6:00 PM and goes until late at night.
- Bring cash. Most of the vendors at the Fish Fry only accept cash.
- Be prepared to wait. The Fish Fry can be very busy, so you may have to wait in line for food and drinks.

- Try a variety of dishes. There are so many different food stalls to choose from, so be sure to try a variety of dishes.
- Don't forget to try a Bajan pepper sauce. Bajan pepper sauces are known for being flavorful and spicy.
- Enjoy the atmosphere! The Oistins Fish Fry is a great place to experience Barbadian culture. Relax, enjoy the food and music, and soak up the atmosphere.

Here are some of the most popular dishes to try at the Oistins Fish Fry: Grilled mahi mahi, Fried flying fish, Lobster creole, Cou cou, Macaroni pie, Coleslaw and Bajan pepper sauce.

Rum Tours, A Taste of Barbados

Rum tours are a popular tourist activity in Barbados, and for good reason. Barbados is known for its world-class rum, and there are a number of distilleries on the island that offer tours and tastings.

Rum tours are a great way to learn about the history and production of rum. You'll see how the rum is made, from the sugarcane harvest to the distillation and ageing process. You'll also get to sample a variety of different rums, from white rum to dark rum to flavored rum.

There are a number of different rum distilleries in Barbados that offer tours, including:

- Mount Gay Rum Distillery, phone (246) 424-6030, cost BDS$35 for adults, BDS$20 for children.

- Foursquare Rum Distillery, phone (246) 423-6201, cost BDS$60 for adults, BDS$30 for children.

- St. Nicholas Abbey, phone (246) 422-4747, cost BDS$50 for adults, BDS$25 for children.

- West Indies Rum Distillery, phone (246) 426-7950, cost BDS$40 for adults, BDS$20 for children.

- Rum Vault Barbados, phone (246) 427-0030, cost BDS$50 for adults, BDS$25 for children.

When choosing a rum tour, be sure to consider your interests. Some distilleries offer tours that are more focused on the history of rum, while others offer tours that are more focused on the production process. Some distilleries also offer tastings of their premium rums, which can be a great way to sample some of the best rums that Barbados has to offer.

Barbadian Drinks

1. Rum Punch: Rum punch is a refreshing and delicious cocktail made with rum, fruit juices, and spices. It is the national drink of Barbados and is enjoyed by locals and tourists alike. Rum punch is typically made with white rum, pineapple juice, orange juice, grapefruit juice, lime juice, and spices such as nutmeg, cinnamon, and cloves.

2. Mauby: Mauby is a bittersweet drink made from the bark of the mauby tree. It is a popular drink in Barbados and other Caribbean islands, and is often enjoyed on a hot day. Mauby is made by boiling the bark of the mauby tree in water with sugar and spices such as cinnamon, cloves, and nutmeg. The drink is then strained and served chilled.

3. **Falernum:** Falernum is a sweet, syrupy liqueur made with rum, sugar, and spices. It is a popular ingredient in cocktails and is also enjoyed on its own. Ingredients: Falernum is made by soaking spices such as ginger, cloves, nutmeg, and allspice in rum. Sugar is then added to the mixture and the falernum is bottled.

4. **Sorrel:** Sorrel is a tart and refreshing drink made from the dried hibiscus flower. It is a popular drink in Barbados during the Christmas season. Sorrel is made by boiling dried hibiscus flowers with water, sugar, and spices such as ginger, cloves, and nutmeg. The drink is then strained and served chilled or hot.

5. **Coconut Water:** Coconut water is a refreshing and hydrating drink that is found inside the coconut fruit. It is a popular drink in Barbados and other tropical countries. Coconut water is 100% natural and contains no added sugar or preservatives.

Barbados is a beautiful island nation in the Caribbean, known for its stunning beaches, crystal-clear waters, and friendly people. It is also home to a number of world-class restaurants, including many luxury establishments.

Where To Eat

Here are five different luxury restaurants in Barbados you can check out:

1. **The Cliff:** The Cliff is a fine-dining restaurant located on a cliff top overlooking the Caribbean Sea. It is known for its stunning views, excellent food, and impeccable service. The Cliff Restaurant, Highway 1, Holetown, St. James, Barbados. The average price of a main course at The Cliff is BDS$150. Phone, (246) 424-0222.

The Cliff's menu features a variety of seafood, meat, and vegetarian dishes, all prepared with fresh, local ingredients. Some of the most popular menu items include the seared scallops with black truffle risotto, the grilled lobster with lemon butter sauce, and the filet mignon with roasted vegetables.

2. The Tides: The Tides is a fine-dining restaurant located on the beach in Holetown. It is known for its romantic atmosphere, excellent food, and impeccable service. The Tides, Holetown, St. James, Barbados. The average price of a main course at The Tides is BDS$120. Phone, (246) 422-2432

The Tides' menu features a variety of seafood, meat, and vegetarian dishes, all prepared with fresh, local ingredients. Some of the most popular menu items include the grilled octopus with chorizo and chickpea salad, the roasted duck breast with cherry confit and foie gras sauce, and the pan-seared scallops with risotto and black truffle.

3. Champers: Champers is a fine-dining restaurant located on the beach in Rockley. It is known for its stunning views, excellent food, and impeccable service. Champers Restaurant, Rockley, St. James, Barbados. The average price of a main course at Champers is BDS$100. Phone, (246) 432-8356

Champers' menu features a variety of seafood, meat, and vegetarian dishes, all prepared with fresh, local ingredients. Some of the most popular menu items include the grilled mahi mahi with lemon butter sauce, the pan-seared scallops with risotto and black truffle, and the filet mignon with roasted vegetables.

4. Primo: Primo is a fine-dining restaurant located in the Sugar Hill Resort. It is known for its elegant atmosphere, excellent food, and impeccable service. Sugar Hill Resort, St. James, Barbados. The average price of a main course at Primo is BDS$130.

Primo's menu features a variety of seafood, meat, and vegetarian dishes, all prepared with fresh, local ingredients. Some of the most popular menu items include the seared scallops with black truffle risotto, the grilled lobster with lemon butter sauce, and the filet mignon with roasted vegetables. Phone: (246) 422-4222

5. Lone Star: Lone Star is a popular restaurant located on the beach in Holetown. It is known for its lively atmosphere, excellent food, and impeccable service. Lone Star Restaurant, Holetown, St. James, Barbados. The average price of a main course at Lone Star is BDS$90.

Lone Star's menu features a variety of seafood, meat, and vegetarian dishes, all prepared with fresh, local ingredients. Some of the most popular menu items include the grilled mahi mahi with lemon butter sauce, the pan-seared scallops with risotto and black truffle, and the filet

Here are 5 different local low budget restaurants in Barbados:

1. Cuz's Fish Stand: Cuz's Fish Stand is a popular spot for fresh seafood at affordable prices. The restaurant is located in a casual setting and offers a variety of seafood dishes, including grilled fish, fried fish, and fish sandwiches. Cuz's Fish Stand is located at 152 Maxwell

Coast Road, Christ Church, Barbados. The average price per food item at Cuz's Fish Stand is BDS$20. Phone (246) 239-1938

2. Just Grillin': Just Grillin' is a popular spot for grilled meats and seafood. The restaurant is located in a casual setting and offers a variety of grilled dishes, including chicken, steak, fish, and shrimp. Just Grillin' is located at 115 Maxwell Coast Road, Christ Church, Barbados. The average price per food item at Just Grillin' is BDS$25. Phone (246) 420-6694

3. Happy Days Cafe: Happy Days Cafe is a popular spot for local Bajan cuisine at affordable prices. The restaurant is located in a casual setting and offers a variety of Bajan dishes, including flying fish and cou cou, roti, and cutters. Happy Days Cafe is located at 333 Martindale's Road, St. Michael, Barbados. The average price per food item at Happy Days Cafe is BDS$15. Phone (246) 425-4515.

4. The Roti Den: The Roti Den is a popular spot for roti, a Caribbean street food made with flatbread and a variety of fillings. The restaurant is located in a casual setting and offers a variety of roti fillings, including chicken, goat, and shrimp. The Roti Den is located at 134 Roebuck Street, Bridgetown, Barbados. The average price per food item at The Roti Den is BDS$10. Phone (246) 261-1223

5. Chillin & Grillin: Chillin & Grillin' is a popular spot for grilled meats and seafood on the south coast of Barbados. The restaurant is located in a casual setting and offers a variety of grilled dishes, including chicken, steak, fish, and shrimp. Chillin & Grillin' is located at 458 Airport Road, Christ Church, Barbados. The average price per food item at Chillin & Grillin' is BDS$25. Phone (246) 428-8627

CHAPTER THREE: THINGS TO DO IN BARBADOS

Barbados, a Caribbean gem, offers a treasure trove of experiences for every traveler. From pristine beaches and lush botanical gardens to historical sites and water sports galore, the island beckons with a diverse array of activities. Whether you seek relaxation, adventure, or cultural immersion, Barbados has it all. In this section, we'll guide you through the unforgettable adventures that await you on this vibrant island.

Hiking in Barbados

Barbados is a beautiful island with a variety of hiking trails to suit all levels of experience. From easy walks along the coast to challenging climbs through the rainforest, there is something for everyone.

Here are some of the best places to go hiking in Barbados:

1. **East Coast:** The east coast of Barbados is home to some of the island's most dramatic scenery, including towering cliffs, secluded beaches, and lush rainforests. Some popular hiking trails on the east coast include the Bathsheba Coastal Walk, the Andromeda Botanic Gardens Trail, and the Codrington College Trail.

2. **Central Highlands:** The central highlands of Barbados are home to the island's highest point, Mount Hillaby, as well as a number of other hills and valleys. Some popular hiking trails in the central highlands include the Mount Hillaby Trail, the Welchman Hall Gully Trail, and the Barclay's Park Trail.

3. **South Coast:** The south coast of Barbados is known for its beautiful beaches and turquoise waters. However, there are also a number of hiking trails in the south coast, including the Boardwalk Trail and the Carlisle Bay Coastal Walk.

When hiking in Barbados, it is important to be prepared. Here are some essential items to bring: Comfortable shoes or hiking boots, Sunscreen, Insect repellent, Water bottle or hydration pack, Snacks, Hat, Sunglasses, Map and compass or GPS device and First-aid kit.

Here are a few insider tips for hiking in Barbados:
- The best time to hike in Barbados is early in the morning or late in the afternoon, when it is cooler.
- Be aware of the weather conditions and avoid hiking in wet or windy weather.
- Let someone know where you are going and when you expect to be back.
- Stay on the marked trails and do not venture off into the bush.
- Be respectful of the wildlife and environment.
- Most of the hiking trails in Barbados are free to access. However, there are a few trails that require a fee, such as the Andromeda Botanic Gardens Trail and the Codrington College Trail.

- Some of the hiking trails in Barbados can be challenging, so it is important to be prepared and to choose a trail that is appropriate for your fitness level.
- There are a number of tour companies in Barbados that offer guided hikes. This can be a good option for those who are new to hiking or who want to learn more about the island's flora and fauna.

Wildlife Encounters

Barbados is a beautiful island with a rich wildlife heritage. From its lush rainforests to its pristine beaches, there are many opportunities to encounter wildlife in Barbados. Here are a few of the best places to have a wildlife encounter in Barbados:

1. **Harrison's Cave:** Harrison's Cave is a stunning limestone cave system with a variety of wildlife, including green monkeys, bats, and cave fish. Visitors can take a guided tour of the caves and learn about the unique wildlife that lives there.

• **Insider tip:** The best time to visit Harrison's Cave is during the day, when the monkeys are most active.

2. Barbados Wildlife Reserve: The Barbados Wildlife Reserve is a nature reserve that is home to a variety of Barbadian wildlife, including monkeys, tortoises, snakes, and parrots. Visitors can explore the reserve at their own pace and see the animals up close.

• **Insider tip:** The best time to visit the Barbados Wildlife Reserve is during the morning, when the animals are most active.

3. Carlisle Bay: Carlisle Bay is a beautiful beach on the south coast of Barbados. The bay is home to a variety of marine life, including sea turtles, tropical fish, and coral reefs. Visitors can snorkel, dive, or swim in the bay and see the marine life up close.

• **Insider tip:** The best time to snorkel or dive in Carlisle Bay is during the morning, when the water is clearest.

4. Andromeda Botanic Gardens: The Andromeda Botanic Gardens is a beautiful botanical garden on the east coast of Barbados. The gardens are home to a variety of tropical plants and flowers, as well as a variety of wildlife, including hummingbirds, butterflies, and tropical birds. Visitors can wander through the gardens at their own pace and enjoy the beauty of the wildlife.

- **Insider tip:** The best time to visit the Andromeda Botanic Gardens is during the morning, when the hummingbirds are most active.

5. Codrington College: Codrington College is a beautiful historic college on the east coast of Barbados. The college grounds are home to a variety of Barbadian wildlife, including green monkeys and tropical birds. Visitors can take a self-guided tour of the college grounds and see the wildlife up close.

- **Insider tip:** The best time to visit Codrington College is during the late afternoon, when the monkeys are most active.

Golfing in Paradise

Barbados is a golfer's paradise, with four world-class golf courses to choose from. The courses offer stunning scenery, challenging layouts, and excellent amenities, making Barbados a perfect destination for a golfing vacation.

Locations where one can go golfing in Barbados:

1. **Sandy Lane Country Club:** The Sandy Lane Country Club is one of the most prestigious golf courses in Barbados. It is a Tom Fazio-designed course that offers stunning views of the Caribbean Sea.

2. **Royal Westmoreland Golf Course:** The Royal Westmoreland Golf Course is another world-class course in Barbados. It is a Robert Trent Jones Jr.-designed course that is known for its challenging layout and beautiful scenery.

3. **Barbados Golf Club:** The Barbados Golf Club is the island's only public golf course. This particular course

presents a challenge that caters to golfers across various proficiency levels.

4. Rockley Golf Club: The Rockley Golf Club is a nine-hole course that is located on the south coast of Barbados. It is a great option for golfers who are looking for a quick and fun round of golf.

The cost of golfing in Barbados varies depending on the course and the time of year. The Sandy Lane Country Club is the most expensive course, with green fees starting at BDS$500. The Royal Westmoreland Golf Course is also expensive, with green fees starting at BDS$400. The Barbados Golf Club is more affordable, with green fees starting at BDS$150. The Rockley Golf Club is the most affordable option, with green fees starting at BDS$50.

Golfing essentials:
1. Golf clubs: You can bring your own golf clubs to Barbados, or you can rent them from one of the golf courses.

2. Golf shoes: Golf shoes are required on all of the golf courses in Barbados.

3. Golf balls: Golf balls can be purchased from the pro shops at the golf courses.

4. Water: It is also important to stay hydrated when golfing in Barbados, so be sure to bring plenty of water with you.

You can purchase golfing essentials from the pro shops at the golf courses in Barbados. You can also rent golf clubs and shoes from the pro shops.

Water Sports

Barbados is a water sports paradise, with its crystal-clear waters, sandy beaches, and consistent trade winds. There is a wide variety of water sports to choose from in Barbados, including:

1. Surfing: Barbados is home to some of the best surfing spots in the Caribbean, including Soup Bowl and Brandon's Beach. The best time to surf in Barbados is during the winter months (November to April), when the waves are larger and more consistent.

2. Windsurfing and kitesurfing: Barbados is also a great place to go windsurfing and kitesurfing, thanks to its consistent trade winds. The best spots for windsurfing and kitesurfing are Silver Sands Beach and Carlisle Bay.

3. Jet skiing: Jet skiing is a popular water sport in Barbados, and there are a number of operators that offer rentals and tours. The best places to go jet skiing in Barbados are the west coast and south coast beaches.

4. Parasailing: Parasailing is a great way to see Barbados from a different perspective. There are a number of operators that offer parasailing tours from the west coast and south coast beaches.

5. Scuba diving and snorkeling: Barbados is home to a number of beautiful coral reefs, making it a great place to go scuba diving and snorkeling. There are a number of operators that offer scuba diving and snorkeling tours from the west coast and south coast beaches.

The cost of water sports in Barbados varies depending on the activity and the operator. However, most water sports are relatively affordable, especially when compared to other Caribbean destinations.

Other necessary information for tourists:

- Book your water sports activities in advance, especially if you are visiting during peak season.
- Be aware of the currents and tides.
- If you are a beginner, be sure to take lessons from a qualified instructor.
- Most water sports operators in Barbados accept credit cards.
- It is a good idea to tip your water sports instructor or guide.

- Be sure to check the weather forecast before participating in water sports.
- If you have any medical conditions, be sure to inform your water sports instructor or guide.

Attend Festivals and Events

1. **Crop Over Festival:** Crop Over is Barbados' premier summer festival, and it is one of the most popular festivals in the Caribbean. The festival celebrates the end of the sugarcane harvest and features a variety of events, including parades, concerts, and food fairs.

Crop Over begins in early June and runs until early August. The festival culminates in the Grand Kadooment parade on the first Monday in August. The Grand Kadooment parade is a massive street party with thousands of people dressed in colorful costumes and dancing to the rhythm of calypso and soca music.

Other popular Crop Over events include:

● **Opening Gala and Ceremonial Delivery of the Last Canes:** This event marks the official start of the Crop Over season and features a parade of costumed revelers, as well as the crowning of the King and Queen of the Crop.

● **Sweetest Bands Show:** This event showcases the best masquerade bands in Barbados, and it is a must-see for any Crop Over visitor.

● **Cohobblopot:** This event is a celebration of Bajan culture and features food stalls, music, and dancing.

● **Bridgetown Market:** This market is held every Saturday during the Crop Over season and features a variety of vendors selling food, drinks, and souvenirs.

2. Holetown Festival: The Holetown Festival is a week-long festival that celebrates the arrival of the first English settlers to Barbados in 1625. The festival is held in the town of Holetown, where the settlers first landed.

The Holetown Festival is held in the town of Holetown in late February and early March. The Holetown Festival features a variety of events, including reenactments of historical events, concerts, and food fairs. The festival also features a number of cultural exhibits, including a display of traditional Bajan crafts and a showcase of Bajan cuisine.

Some of the most popular Holetown Festival events include:

• **Reenactment of the Landing of the First Settlers:** This reenactment takes place on the first day of the festival and features a group of actors dressed as the first English settlers to Barbados landing on the beach in Holetown.

• **Holetown Festival Concert:** This concert features a variety of Barbadian artists, including calypsonians, soca singers, and bands.

- **Holetown Festival Food Fair:** This food fair features a variety of food stalls selling Barbadian cuisine, as well as international cuisine.

- **Holetown Festival Artisan Market:** This market features a variety of vendors selling handmade crafts and souvenirs.

3. Reggae Festival: The Barbados Reggae Festival is an annual festival that celebrates reggae music and culture. The festival is typically held in March or April and features a variety of reggae artists, both local and international. The festival also includes food and drink stalls, as well as arts and crafts vendors.

On the day of the festival, attendees can expect to hear a variety of reggae music, from classic hits to new releases. There are also typically several stages, so there is always something to see. In addition to the music, there is also a variety of food and drink available, as well as arts and crafts vendors.

The Barbados Reggae Festival is a great way to experience the best of reggae music and culture. The festival is also a great place to meet new people and have a good time.

4. Food and Rum Festival: The Barbados Food and Rum Festival is an annual festival that celebrates the island's cuisine and rum. The festival is typically held in November and features a variety of food stalls, cooking demonstrations, and rum tastings. The event features live performances of music and various forms of entertainment.

On the day of the festival, attendees can expect to try a variety of Barbadian food, from traditional dishes like flying fish and cou cou to more modern fare. There are also typically several cooking demonstrations, where attendees can learn how to make some of their favorite Barbadian dishes. In addition to the food, there are also a variety of rum tastings, where attendees can sample some of the best rums that Barbados has to offer. The festival also includes live music and entertainment, making it a great place to spend a day or evening.

The Barbados Food and Rum Festival is a great way to experience the best of Barbadian cuisine and rum. The festival is also a great place to learn about Barbadian culture and meet new people.

Family-Friendly Fun

1. Splashdown Water Park: Splashdown Water Park is a family-friendly water park located in Christ Church, Barbados. The park offers an array of water slides, pools, and diverse attractions suitable for individuals of all age groups.

Activities that can be done there:

1. Ride the water slides, including the Kamikaze, the Bullet Bowl, and the Lazy River.
2. Swim in the pools, including the main pool, the wave pool, and the children's pool.
3. Play games on the water playground.

4. Unwind in the comfortable beach chairs and bask in the warmth of the sun's rays.

Other Necessary information for tourists:

- Cost: Adults BDS$65, children (3-12 years old) BDS$35 and children under 3 years old is free
- Operational hours: Monday to Saturday 9:00 AM to 5:00 PM and sunday 10:00 AM to 5:00 PM
- Phone number: (246) 428-1000
- Splashdown Water Park is open year-round.
- The park is wheelchair accessible.
- There are changing rooms, showers, and lockers available on site.
- Food and drinks are available for purchase at the park.

2. **Barbados Wildlife Reserve:** The Barbados Wildlife Reserve is a wildlife park located in St. Michael, Barbados. The park is home to a variety of animals, including monkeys, turtles, snakes, and birds.

Activities that can be done there:

1. Observe the wildlife from a close vantage point and gain insights into their natural environments.

2. Take a guided tour of the park.

3. Feed the monkeys.

4. Visit the reptile house.

5. See the bird show.

Other necessary information for tourists:

- Cost: Adults BDS$25   children (3-12 years old) BDS$12.50 and children under 3 years old is free

- Operational hours: 9:00 AM to 4:00 PM daily

- Phone number: (246) 433-8558

- The Barbados Wildlife Reserve is open year-round.

- The park is wheelchair accessible.

- There are changing rooms and showers available on site.

- Food and drinks are available for purchase at the park.

3. Atlantis Submarines: Atlantis Submarines is a submarine tour company that offers tours of the coral reefs off the coast of Barbados.

Activities that can be done there:

1. Explore the breathtaking coral reefs with an underwater submarine excursion.

2. See the marine life up close, including fish, turtles, and coral reefs.

3. Learn about the marine ecosystem.

Other necessary information for tourists:

- Cost: Adults BDS$275, children (3-12 years old) BDS$150 and children under 3 years old is free

- Operational hours: Tours depart daily at 10:00 AM, 12:00 PM, and 2:00 PM.

- Phone number: (246) 426-4445

- Atlantis Submarines tours are suitable for all ages.

4. **Barbados Garrison:** The Barbados Garrison is a historic military complex located in the heart of Bridgetown. The Garrison was designated a UNESCO World Heritage Site in 2006. The Garrison is a great place to visit for families with children of all ages. There are a number of activities and attractions to keep everyone entertained.

The Barbados Garrison is located in the heart of Bridgetown, just a short walk from the cruise ship terminal. The Garrison is easy to access by public transportation or taxi.

There are a number of activities and attractions to enjoy at the Barbados Garrison, including:

1. The Garrison Savannah: The Garrison Savannah is a large park that is located in the center of the Garrison. The Savannah is a great place to relax and have a picnic. It is also a popular spot for flying kites and playing cricket.

2. The Barbados Defence Force Museum: The Barbados Defence Force Museum is a museum that tells the story of the Barbados Defence Force. The museum has a variety of exhibits on the history of the Barbados Defence Force, as well as its uniforms, weapons, and equipment. The price is BDS$10 for adults, BDS$5 for children.

The Barbados Garrison is open to the public from 8:00 AM to 5:00 PM, seven days a week.

Other Necessary Information for Tourists:

- The Barbados Garrison is a wheelchair-accessible site.
- There are restrooms available at the Garrison and at Splashdown Water Park.
- There are a number of restaurants and cafes located near the Garrison.
- There is a gift shop located at the Barbados Museum.
- The best time to visit the Barbados Garrison is during the off-season (May to November), when the weather is cooler and there are fewer crowds.
- There are a number of shady areas in the Garrison where you can rest and have a picnic.
- Be sure to check the operational hours of the activities and attractions that you want to visit before you go.
- If you are visiting with a group, be sure to book your tickets in advance.

5. Barbados Museum Kids Zone: The Barbados Museum Kids Zone is a family-friendly interactive gallery that teaches children about the island's history, culture, and natural environment. The gallery is divided into different sections, each with its own unique activities and exhibits.

The Barbados Museum Kids Zone is located at the Barbados Museum and Historical Society, St. Ann's Garrison, Bridgetown, Barbados.:

Some of the activities that children can do at the Barbados Museum Kids Zone include:

1. Learning about the history of Barbados through interactive exhibits.

2. Exploring the island's natural environment through hands-on activities.

3. Discovering Barbadian culture through music, dance, and art.

4. Playing dress-up in traditional Barbadian clothing

5. Reading stories about Barbadian history and culture

6. Participating in workshops and special events

Other necessary information for tourists:

● **Cost:** The admission fee to the Barbados Museum Kids Zone is BDS$12.50 for children and BDS$20 for adults. A special discount offer is available for groups consisting of 10 or more individuals.

● **Operational hours:** The Barbados Museum Kids Zone is open from Monday to Friday from 9:00 AM to 4:30 PM and on Saturdays from 9:00 AM to 1:00 PM.

● Phone number: The phone number for the Barbados Museum is (246) 427-0909.

● Photography is permitted in the gallery.

● The museum offers a variety of educational programs for children of all ages.

Shopping and Souvenirs

Barbados is a great place to shop for souvenirs and keepsakes, with a variety of markets and shopping locations to choose from. Here are some suggestions to enhance your shopping experience:

1. Be prepared to bargain: Bargaining is common in Barbados, especially at the markets. Feel free to negotiate with the sellers in order to secure a more favorable price.

2. Shop around: Don't purchase the initial souvenir you come across. Take your time and shop around to compare prices and find the best deals.

3. Support local businesses: When shopping for souvenirs, try to support local businesses whenever possible. This will help to support the Barbadian economy and ensure that you are getting authentic souvenirs.

Here are a few of the most popular markets and shopping locations in Barbados:

1. Pelican Craft Village: his popular market is located in Bridgetown and features a variety of stalls selling souvenirs, crafts, and local produce.

2. Chattel Village: This charming village is located in Holetown and features a collection of chattel houses, which are traditional Barbadian cottages. The chattel houses sell a variety of souvenirs, crafts, and clothing.

3. Broad Street: This busy street in Bridgetown is lined with shops selling everything from souvenirs to clothing to electronics.

4. Cave Shepherd: This department store is located in Bridgetown and sells a wide variety of goods, including souvenirs, clothing, and cosmetics.

Here are a few souvenir ideas:

1. Flying fish: The flying fish is the national symbol of Barbados, so it's no surprise that flying fish souvenirs are very popular. You can find flying fish t-shirts, hats, jewelry, and other trinkets at most markets and shops in Barbados.

2. Bajan rum: Barbados is known for its world-class rum, so be sure to pick up a bottle or two as a souvenir.

You can find Bajan rum at most markets and shops in Barbados, as well as at the distilleries themselves.

3. Handmade crafts: Barbados has a rich tradition of craftsmanship, and there are a number of talented artisans who create beautiful handmade crafts. You can find handmade pottery, jewelry, woodwork, and other crafts at markets and shops throughout the island.

4. Local produce: Barbados produces a variety of delicious fruits and vegetables, so be sure to pick up some local produce to take home with you. You can find local produce at markets and shops throughout the island.

Here are a few insider tips for shopping in Barbados:

● The best time to bargain is in the afternoon. Vendors are more likely to negotiate on prices in the afternoon, when they are less busy.

● Be aware of the exchange rate. Barbados uses the Barbadian dollar (BDS). Be sure to check the exchange rate before you shop so that you know how much you are spending.

● Use cash. Many vendors in Barbados only accept cash. It's a good idea to have some cash on hand when you go shopping.

● Ask about discounts. Many vendors offer discounts for groups or for multiple purchases. Prior to making your purchase, it's essential to inquire about potential discounts.

Relaxation and Wellness

Barbados is a great place to relax and de-stress, with its beautiful beaches, lush rainforests, and tranquil atmosphere. There are a number of different options available for tourists who are looking for a relaxing and wellness-oriented vacation.

1. Spa Retreats: There are a number of different spa retreats available in Barbados, offering a variety of treatments and services. Here are a few of the most popular spa retreats on the island:

- **The Spa at Sandy Lane:** This luxurious spa offers a wide range of treatments, including massages, facials, body wraps, and hydrotherapy. Phone (246) 444-2000

- **The Spa at The Crane:** This world-class spa offers stunning views of the Caribbean Sea and features a variety of treatment rooms, including a couples suite and a hydrotherapy room. Phone (246) 423-6260

- **The Spa at Coral Reef Club:** This intimate spa offers a personalized approach to wellness and features a variety of treatments, including massages, facials, and body wraps. Phone (246) 422-2502

The cost of a spa retreat in Barbados varies depending on the spa, the length of the stay, and the treatments that are selected. However, most spa retreats are relatively affordable, especially when compared to other Caribbean destinations.

2. Yoga and Wellness Centers: There are a number of different yoga and wellness centers in Barbados, offering a variety of classes and workshops. Here are a few of the most popular yoga and wellness centers on the island:

- **Yoga at the Beach Barbados:** This yoga studio offers a variety of yoga classes, including beginner, intermediate, and advanced classes. The studio provides meditation classes and workshops as well. Phone (246) 831-5793

- **The Wellness Connection Barbados:** This wellness center offers a variety of yoga classes, as well as Pilates classes, meditation classes, and nutrition counseling. Phone (246) 255-7373

- **Zen Yoga Barbados:** This yoga studio offers a variety of yoga classes, including Vinyasa yoga, Yin yoga, and restorative yoga. The studio provides meditation classes and workshops as well. Phone (246) 269-5139

The cost of yoga and wellness classes in Barbados varies depending on the studio and the type of class. However, most classes are relatively affordable.

Nightlife and Party

Barbados is known for its vibrant nightlife and lively party scene. There are a number of different bars and clubs to choose from, depending on your musical taste and budget. Here are a few of the most popular nightlife spots in Barbados:

1. Harbour Lights: This popular nightclub is located in Bridgetown and offers a variety of music genres, including soca, reggae, and hip hop. The club also has a large outdoor patio with stunning views of the Caribbean Sea.

2. Coconuts: This lively nightclub is located in St. Lawrence Gap and is known for its energetic atmosphere and friendly staff. The club offers a variety of music genres, including soca, reggae, and dancehall.

3. Reggae Lounge: This laid-back bar is located in St. Lawrence Gap and offers a variety of reggae music. The bar also has a large outdoor patio where you can relax and enjoy a drink.

4. The Cliff: This upscale bar and restaurant is located in St. James and offers stunning views of the Caribbean Sea. The bar offers a variety of cocktails and wines, as well as live music on select nights.

5. Oistins Fish Fry: This popular fish fry is held every Friday evening in the village of Oistins. The fish fry features a variety of food stalls selling fresh seafood, as well as bars selling beer and cocktails. There is also live music and entertainment.

CHAPTER FOUR: DAY TRIPS AND EXCURSIONS

While the heart of Barbados lies in its captivating beaches and charming towns, the island's allure extends far beyond. Day trips and excursions offer an opportunity to explore the diverse landscapes, historical sites, and hidden treasures that make Barbados truly extraordinary. From rugged coastlines to lush botanical gardens, every venture promises a new adventure. In this section, we'll guide you through the best day trips and excursions for an enriching experience beyond the shores.

Island Safari

Embark on an exhilarating journey with Island Safari, an immersive day trip that takes you deep into the heart of Barbados' uncharted territories. Here's what you need to know:

Island Safari tours depart from various locations across the island, including Bridgetown, the South Coast, and the West Coast. Exact departure points are provided upon booking.

The tours take you to the rugged interior of Barbados, providing a unique perspective of the island's diverse landscapes. The starting points are within a 30-minute drive from major tourist areas.

Island Safari offers complimentary pick-up and drop-off services from most hotels and accommodations on the island. Alternatively, guests can arrange their own transportation to the designated departure point.

What Can Be Done During the Tour:

1. Off-Road Adventure: Climb aboard a specially designed 4x4 vehicle, and venture off the beaten path into the heart of Barbados' natural wonders.

2. Scenic Views: Marvel at breathtaking vistas from elevated viewpoints, offering panoramic views of the island's coastline and lush interior.

3. Historical Insights: Learn about the island's rich history and culture from knowledgeable tour guides who share fascinating anecdotes along the way.

4. Wildlife Encounters: Keep an eye out for Barbados' unique flora and fauna, including tropical birds and, if you're lucky, the elusive green monkeys.

Other necessary information for tourists:

- The Island Safari tour lasts about 5 hours.
- The tour is suitable for all ages.
- The tour is conducted in English.
- The cost of the tour is BDS$35 for adults and BDS$20 for children.
- Island Safari offers a variety of tour options, including half-day and full-day adventures, each providing a different perspective of Barbados' beauty.
- Comfortable clothing, closed-toe shoes, and sun protection are recommended for the tour. Water and light refreshments are typically provided.
- Website: www.islandsafari.bb
- Email: info@islandsafari.bb Phone: +1 246-429-5337

- It's advisable to book in advance, especially during peak tourist seasons, to secure your spot on the tour.
- Island Safari tours are led by experienced guides who ensure safety and provide an engaging and informative experience.

Catamaran Cruises

Catamaran cruises are a popular day trip from Barbados, offering a relaxing and scenic way to experience the Caribbean Sea. Catamarans are large, two-hulled boats that are very stable and comfortable, making them ideal for day trips.

There are a number of different catamaran cruise operators in Barbados, offering a variety of different itineraries. Most cruises depart from Bridgetown, the capital of Barbados.

Here are some of the popular catamaran cruise operators in Barbados and their phone numbers:

- Tiami Catamaran Cruises: (246) 430-0900
- Cool Runnings Catamaran Cruises: (246) 436-0911
- Wasn't Me Catamaran Cruises: (246) 262-3792
- Silver Moon Catamaran Cruises: (246) 435-5285
- Jammin' Catamaran Cruises: (246) 416-1310
- Island Magic Catamaran Cruises: (246) 424-4100
- Chillin & Grillin' Catamaran Cruises: (246) 428-8627

Here are a few of the most popular locations that are visited on catamaran cruises from Barbados:

- **Carlisle Bay:** This beautiful bay is located on the west coast of Barbados and is known for its crystal-clear waters and white-sand beaches. Carlisle Bay is a popular spot for swimming, snorkeling, and sunbathing.

- **Holetown:** This historic town is located on the west coast of Barbados and is known for its charming shops, restaurants, and art galleries. Holetown is also a popular spot for snorkeling and swimming.

- **Paynes Bay:** This secluded beach is located on the west coast of Barbados and is known for its calm waters and soft sand. Paynes Bay is a popular spot for swimming, sunbathing, and relaxing.

- **Sandy Lane Bay:** This luxury beach is located on the west coast of Barbados and is known for its white sand and turquoise waters. Sandy Lane Bay is a popular spot for swimming, sunbathing, and people-watching.

- **South Coast:** The south coast of Barbados is known for its lively atmosphere and beautiful beaches. Some of the most popular beaches on the south coast include Accra Beach, Dover Beach, and Worthing Beach. These beaches are all popular spots for swimming, sunbathing, and water sports.

All of the locations listed above are located within a short sailing distance of Barbados. The sailing time to each location will vary depending on the wind conditions and the itinerary of the catamaran cruise.

The best way to get to a catamaran cruise is to book a tour with one of the many operators in Barbados. There are a number of different operators to choose from, offering a variety of different itineraries and prices.

Once you are on board the catamaran, there are a number of different things that you can do. Most cruises include swimming, snorkeling, and sunbathing. Certain cruise packages may also offer lunch, snacks, and beverages as part of the experience. Some cruises also offer additional activities, such as fishing, jet skiing, and parasailing.

Hunte's Gardens

Hunte's Gardens is a beautiful and unique tropical garden located in the St. Joseph Parish of Barbados. The garden is known for its lush greenery, variety of flowers, and stunning waterfall. Hunte's Gardens is a popular day trip destination for tourists, offering a relaxing and scenic way to experience the natural beauty of Barbados.

Hunte's Gardens is located in the St. Joseph Parish of Barbados, approximately 15 kilometers from the capital city of Bridgetown. The garden is situated in a rural area, surrounded by sugarcane fields and hills.

Hunte's Gardens is located within a short driving distance of most major tourist destinations in Barbados. The drive from Bridgetown to Hunte's Gardens takes approximately 20-30 minutes.

The best way to get to Hunte's Gardens is by car. There is a small parking lot located on the premises of the garden. If you are not driving, you can also take a taxi or bus to the garden.

Once you arrive at Hunte's Gardens, you can take a self-guided tour of the garden. The garden has been segmented into various sections, each boasting its distinct and individual characteristics. Some of the highlights of the garden include:

- **The waterfall:** The waterfall is the centerpiece of Hunte's Gardens and is a popular spot for taking photos.

- **The Koi pond:** The Koi pond is home to a variety of colorful Koi fish.

- **The rose garden:** The rose garden features a variety of roses, including traditional roses and exotic varieties.

- **The orchid house:** The orchid house features a variety of orchids, including rare and endangered varieties.

- **The hummingbird garden:** The hummingbird garden is home to a variety of hummingbirds.

In addition to touring the garden, you can also enjoy a light lunch or snack at the garden's cafe. The cafe offers a variety of sandwiches, salads, and drinks.

Other Necessary Information for Tourists

- Hunte's Gardens is open from Tuesday to Sunday from 9:00 AM to 4:00 PM.
- Admission to the garden is BDS$30 for adults and BDS$15 for children.

- There is a small gift shop located on the premises of the garden.
- Bring a camera to capture all of the amazing scenery.

- Take your time and savor the beauty of the garden. There is an abundance of sightseeing and things to admire.
- Be sure to visit the hummingbird garden. It is a truly magical experience to see these tiny birds up close.
- Have lunch or a snack at the garden's cafe. The cuisine is exquisite, and the ambiance is stunning.
- Purchase a souvenir from the gift shop to remember your day trip to Hunte's Gardens.

CHAPTER FIVE: ESSENTIAL TRAVEL INFORMATION

Before you set out on your Barbados escapade, it's essential to have a handle on practical travel details. From safety to transportation tips, this section provides you with the vital information you need for a smooth and enjoyable journey.

Getting Around, Transportation Tips and Guide

Barbados is a relatively small island, making it easy to get around. There are a variety of transportation options available to visitors, including buses, taxis, rental cars, and scooters.

1. **Buses:** The bus system in Barbados is extensive and affordable. Buses run throughout the island and connect all of the major tourist destinations. There are two types of buses in Barbados: regular buses and route taxis. Regular buses are blue and have a ZM license plate. Route taxis are white and have a ZM license plate.

To catch a bus, simply flag one down on the side of the road. The fare is BDS$3.50 for adults and BDS$1.75 for children. You can pay the driver in cash.

2. Taxis: Taxis are another convenient way to get around Barbados. Taxis are readily available at all major tourist destinations and can be hailed on the side of the road or called by phone.

The taxi fare in Barbados is based on a zone system. The fare for a zone-to-zone trip is BDS$10. For a trip that crosses more than one zone, the fare is BDS$15. You have the option to settle your taxi fare with either cash or a credit card.

3. Rental Cars: If you want the freedom to explore Barbados at your own pace, you can rent a car.

Here are the top 3 car rental companies in Barbados and their phone numbers:

1. Sixt: (246) 425-0124

2. Stoutes Car Rental: (246) 428-3549

3. Autounion Car Rental: (246) 260-9863

These companies offer a variety of car rental options, including economy cars, SUVs, and vans. They also offer a variety of pick-up and drop-off locations, including the airport, hotels, and cruise ship terminals.

When selecting a car rental provider, it is crucial to engage in price comparisons and pursue customer reviews. Additionally, it is imperative to confirm that the chosen company possesses the necessary licenses and insurance coverage.

Here are some things to keep in mind when renting a car in Barbados:

- You must be at least 25 years old to rent a car in Barbados.
- You will need a valid driver's license.
- You will need to purchase a temporary driver's license for Barbados. The cost of a temporary driver's license is BDS$20.

• You will need to have a credit card to pay for the car rental.

4. Scooters: Scooters are a popular way to get around Barbados, especially among younger visitors. Scooters are relatively inexpensive to rent and easy to manoeuvre.

Here are the top 3 scooter rental companies in Barbados and their phone numbers:

1. Scoot Barbados
Phone Number: (246) 434-1393
Address: 133 Dover Road, St. Michael

2. Scoot a Boogie Barbados
Phone Number: (246) 422-1660
Address: 173B Worthing Main Road, Worthing, Christ Church

3. Scooter World Barbados
Phone Number: (246) 422-2122

Address: 472 Worthing Main Road, Worthing, Christ Church

These companies offer a variety of scooters to rent, including gas-powered scooters and electric scooters. They also offer a variety of rental packages, including one-day rentals and weekly rentals.

When renting a scooter in Barbados, be sure to ask about the following: The cost of the rental, The insurance options, the fuel policy, the delivery and pick-up options and the safety requirements.

However, it is important to be aware of the traffic conditions in Barbados before renting a scooter. The traffic can be heavy and there are many narrow roads. It is also important to wear a helmet when riding a scooter.

Here are a few insider tips for moving around Barbados:

164

- **Buy a bus pass:** If you plan on using the bus system frequently, you can save money by buying a bus pass. Bus passes are available for one day, seven days, or one month.

- **Negotiate with taxi drivers:** Taxi drivers in Barbados are willing to negotiate on the fare. If you are taking a taxi to a popular tourist destination, be sure to negotiate the fare with the driver before getting in the taxi.

- **Be aware of the traffic conditions:** The traffic in Barbados can be heavy, especially during the peak season. Ensure you schedule your travel time appropriately.

- **Drive defensively:** The roads in Barbados are narrow and winding. It is important to drive defensively and be aware of the other drivers on the road.

- **Be careful when riding a scooter:** The traffic in Barbados can be heavy and there are many narrow roads.

It is important to be careful and wear a helmet when riding a scooter.

Accommodation, Where to Stay

Barbados is a beautiful island with a wide range of accommodation options to choose from, depending on your budget and preferences. Here are a few of the best places to stay in Barbados:

1. The Sandy Lane: This luxurious resort is located on the west coast of Barbados and offers stunning views of the Caribbean Sea. The resort features a variety of amenities, including a private beach, multiple pools, a spa, tennis courts, fitness center, kids' club, multiple restaurants and bars and a golf course. The Sandy Lane is located approximately 30 minutes from Grantley Adams International Airport. You have the option to either use a taxi or bus service or arrange for a private transfer. An accommodation costs about US$500+ per night.

- Website: https://www.sandylane.com/, Phone: (246) 424-4000, Star reviews: 5 stars on TripAdvisor and Google.

2. The Crane Resort: This iconic resort is located on the south coast of Barbados and is known for its clifftop location and stunning views of the Atlantic Ocean. The resort features a variety of amenities, including a private beach, multiple pools, a spa, tennis courts, fitness center, kids' club, multiple restaurants and bars and a golf course. The Crane Resort is located approximately 20 minutes from Grantley Adams International Airport. You have the option to either use a taxi or bus service or arrange for a private transfer. An accommodation costs about US$500+ per night.

- Website: https://www.thecrane.com/, Phone: (246) 423-6220, Star reviews: 4.5 stars on TripAdvisor and Google.

3. Fairmont Royal Pavilion: This elegant resort is located on the west coast of Barbados and is known for its white-sand beach and crystal-clear waters. The resort

167

features a variety of amenities, including multiple pools, a spa, and a kids' club. Fairmont Royal Pavilion is located approximately 30 minutes from Grantley Adams International Airport. You have the option to either use a taxi or bus service or arrange for a private transfer. Accommodation cost $200-500 per night.

- Website: https://www.fairmont.com/barbados/, Phone: (246) 422-4356, Star reviews: 4.5 stars on TripAdvisor and Google

4. Hilton Barbados Resort: This family-friendly resort is located on the south coast of Barbados and is known for its spacious rooms, multiple pools, and kids' club. The resort also features a private beach and a variety of dining options. Hilton Barbados Resort is located approximately 20 minutes from Grantley Adams International Airport. Taxis are available outside of the airport. The fare to the Hilton Barbados Resort is approximately BDS$50.00. Accommodation cost $200-500 per night.

- Phone: (246) 426-0200, Website: https://www.hilton.com/en/hotels/bgihihh-hilton-barbados-resort/ , Star rating: 4.5 stars.

5. Mango Bay: This boutique hotel is located on the west coast of Barbados and is known for its intimate setting and personalized service. The hotel features a private beach, a pool, and a spa. Mango Bay is located approximately 30 minutes from Grantley Adams International Airport. Taxis are available outside of the airport. The fare to Mango Bay is approximately BDS$75.00. Accommodation cost about US$200 or less per night.

- Phone: (246) 422-4555, Website: https://mangobaybarbados.com/ ,Star rating: 4.5 stars.

6. Cobblers Cove: This charming hotel is located on the west coast of Barbados and is known for its colonial-style architecture and oceanfront location. The hotel features a private beach, a pool, and a restaurant. Cobblers Cove is located approximately 30 minutes from Grantley Adams International Airport. You have the option to either use a taxi or bus service or arrange for a private transfer. Accommodation cost about US$200 or less per night.

- Phone: (246) 422-4109, Website: https://www.cobblerscove.com/ , Star rating: 5 stars.

7. The Sugar Bay Hotel: This beachfront hotel is located in Maxwell, Christ Church, on the south coast of Barbados and is known for its family-friendly atmosphere and multiple pools. The hotel also features a private beach and a variety of dining options. The taxi ride from the airport to The Sugar Bay Hotel takes approximately 15 minutes and costs around $25. There is a public bus that runs from the airport to Maxwell. The bus ride takes approximately 30 minutes and costs $3.50.

- Price range per night: $150-$250
- Phone number: (246) 424-4090
- Website: https://www.sugarbaybarbados.com/
- Star reviews: TripAdvisor 4 stars, Google 4.2 stars

8. Turtle Beach by Elegant Hotels: This all-inclusive resort is located in Oistins, Christ Church, on the south coast of Barbados and is known for its stunning beach and multiple pools. The resort also features a variety of dining options and a kids' club. The taxi ride from the airport to Turtle Beach by Elegant Hotels takes approximately 15 minutes and costs around $25. There is a public bus that runs from the airport to Oistins. The bus ride takes approximately 30 minutes and costs $3.50.

- Price range per night: $250-$350
- Phone number: (246) 428-7141
- Website: https://all-inclusive.marriott.com/turtle-beach-by-elegant -hotels
- Star reviews: TripAdvisor 4.5 stars, Google 4.3 stars

9. The Bougainvillea Beach Resort: This affordable resort is located on the south coast of Barbados and is known for its beachfront location and multiple pools. The resort also features a variety of dining options and a kids' club. The taxi ride from the airport to The Bougainvillea Beach Resort takes approximately 15 minutes and costs around $25. There is a public bus that runs from the airport to Maxwell. The bus ride takes approximately 30 minutes and costs $3.50.

- Price range per night: $100-$200
- Phone number: (246) 424-4100
- Website: https://www.bougainvilleabarbados.com/

Star reviews: TripAdvisor 4 stars, Google 4.1 stars

Here are a few insider tips for choosing accommodation in Barbados:

- **Consider your budget:** Accommodation prices in Barbados can vary widely, depending on the time of year and the type of accommodation you choose. Be sure to set a budget before you start looking for accommodation.

- **Think about your location:** Barbados is a relatively small island, but it is important to consider where you want to stay. The west coast is known for its beautiful beaches and luxurious resorts, while the south coast is known for its lively nightlife and family-friendly atmosphere.

- **Consider your amenities:** Some hotels and resorts offer a wider range of amenities than others. Be sure to consider the amenities that are important to you, such as a private beach, multiple pools, a spa, and a kids' club.

- **Read reviews:** Before you book your accommodation, be sure to read reviews from other guests. This can assist you in gaining a clearer understanding of what to expect.

Free Things to Do in Barbados

Barbados, with its natural beauty and vibrant culture, offers a plethora of experiences that won't cost you a dime. Here are some free things to do in Barbados:

1. Hit the Beaches: Of course, no trip to Barbados would be complete without spending some time at the beach. And the best part is, many of the beaches in Barbados are free to access. Some popular beaches include Carlisle Bay, Accra Beach, and Dover Beach.

2. Explore Bridgetown: Bridgetown, the capital of Barbados, is a UNESCO World Heritage Site. There are a number of free things to do in Bridgetown, such as visiting the Barbados Museum & Historical Society, the Garrison Historic Area, Independence Square and the Chamberlain Bridge.

3. Take a hike: Barbados is home to a number of beautiful hiking trails, many of which are free to use. One popular option is the East Coast Road Trail, which offers stunning views of the Atlantic Ocean. Another option is the Welchman Hall Gully Trail, which winds through a lush rainforest.

4. Visit Hunte's Gardens: While there's an admission fee for guided tours, you can explore the magnificent gardens for free if you prefer to go at your own pace.

5. Animal Flower Cave: While there may be a small fee for a guided tour, the spectacular coastal views and the natural wonder of the cave are yours to enjoy without charge.

6. Sunset at North Point: Head to North Point in St. Lucy and witness a breathtaking sunset over the rugged cliffs and crashing waves.

7. Attend a free event: There are a number of free events held throughout the year in Barbados. For example, the Oistins Fish Fry is a popular weekly event where you can enjoy fresh seafood and live music. Another option is the Crop Over Festival, which is a two-month celebration of Barbadian culture and heritage.

8. Historic Churches and Plantations: Visit some of the island's historic churches, like St. John's Parish Church, or explore the grounds of old sugar plantations, where you can appreciate the island's rich heritage.

9. Explore Speightstown: This charming town offers a glimpse into the local way of life. Stroll along the streets, visit the galleries, and soak in the atmosphere.

10. Visit a botanical garden: Barbados has a number of beautiful botanical gardens, many of which are free to enter. One popular option is Andromeda Botanic Gardens, which features a variety of tropical plants and flowers. Another option is the Barbados Wildlife Reserve, which is home to a variety of native Barbadian animals, including monkeys, tortoises, and snakes

Safety and Health

1. Barbados is a relatively safe island, but it's always important to be aware of your surroundings and take precautions against petty theft. It is advisable to refrain from walking alone during nighttime, particularly in unfamiliar areas.

2. Be careful when swimming at the beach, as the currents can be strong in some areas. It's always best to swim at a beach that has lifeguards on duty.

3. Be aware of the negative effects of staying too long under the sun. Apply sunscreen liberally and reapply often, especially if you're spending time outdoors.

4. Drink bottled water instead of tap water, as the tap water may not be safe to drink.

5. Make sure you're up-to-date on all of your vaccinations before you travel to Barbados. Some recommended vaccinations include measles, mumps, and rubella (MMR), tetanus, diphtheria, and pertussis (Tdap), and hepatitis A and B.

6. Remember to carry a basic first-aid kit to address any minor injuries that may occur.

7. Be aware of the symptoms of mosquito-borne diseases such as dengue fever and Zika virus. Take precautions against mosquito bites by using insect repellent and wearing long sleeves and pants at night.

8. If you become ill while in Barbados, seek medical attention immediately.

9. If you plan on renting a car or using public transportation, familiarize yourself with local traffic rules and road conditions. Always wear seatbelts, and exercise caution when driving, especially at night.

10. Cross the street at crosswalks and be careful of traffic, especially when crossing busy roads.

11. Only take taxis from licensed taxi stands or from hotels and restaurants and make sure the taxi driver uses the meter. Agree on a fare with the driver before getting into the taxi and don't get into a taxi if there are other people in the car that you don't know.

12. When using a bus, be aware of your surroundings and keep an eye on your belongings. Don't carry large amounts of cash or valuables with you and be careful when getting on and off the bus. If you're traveling with children, keep them close to you.

13. If you are renting a car, drive defensively and be aware of the other drivers on the road. The speed limit in Barbados is 60 km/h (37 mph) in urban areas and 80 km/h (50 mph) in rural areas. Be aware of the narrow and winding roads in Barbados. Don't drink and drive. The legal blood alcohol limit in Barbados is 0.08% and park in well-lit areas and don't leave valuables in your car.

14. Make sure the hotel you finally choose to stay in is secured and in a secured environment, make sure your door is locked when you enter or head out of your room and I advice you to have the security contact of the hotel as well.

15. Familiarize yourself with local emergency numbers and make a note of the nearest medical facilities and contact information. Here are some emergency contacts in Barbados:
- Police: 211
- Fire: 311

- Ambulance: 511

- Coast Guard: 427-8819

- Queen Elizabeth Hospital: 436-6450

- US Embassy: (246) 431-0225

- Canadian High Commission: (246) 429-6500

- UK High Commission: (246) 429-6690

112 is the universal emergency number in Barbados. It will connect you to the closest emergency service, regardless of whether you need the police, fire department, or ambulance.

Language and Etiquette

The official language of Barbados is English. However, many Barbadians also speak Bajan, a Creole language that is a mix of English, African languages, and Portuguese. Bajan is often spoken in informal settings, such as among friends and family.

Barbadians are generally friendly and welcoming people. Here are a few tips on etiquette in Barbados:

1. Greetings: Barbadians typically greet each other with a handshake. When greeting someone older or in a position of authority, it is customary to say "Good morning, sir" or "Good morning, ma'am."

2. Addressing people: It is customary to address people by their title and last name, unless you know them well. You can also use the Bajan greeting "Howzit?" to casually greet friends and family.

3. Table manners: Barbadians are generally polite and well-mannered at the table. It is a common practice to refrain from eating until everyone at the table has been served. Always remember to express your gratitude to your host or hostess for the delicious meal.

4. Tipping: Tipping is not customary in Barbados, but it is appreciated for good service. You can tip a few dollars for taxi drivers, waiters, and waitresses.

5. Dress code: Barbadians are generally conservative in their dress code. It is best to avoid wearing revealing clothing, especially when visiting religious sites.

6. Cultural Sensitivity: Respecting the customs and traditions of the local culture is of great significance. Avoid discussing sensitive topics like politics or religion, and refrain from taking photos without permission, especially in private or religious spaces.

Budgeting and Money Saving Tips

Barbados is a beautiful island with something to offer everyone, but it can also be a bit expensive. However, there are ways to save money on a Barbados vacation without sacrificing your enjoyment. Here are a few tips and recommendations:

Budgeting

Before you go on your trip, it's important to create a budget. This will enable you to monitor your expenses effectively and ensure that you stay within your budget. Here are a few tips for creating a budget:

- **Estimate your costs:** This includes the cost of transportation, accommodation, food, activities, and souvenirs.
- **Set a daily spending limit:** This will help you to stay on track and avoid overspending.
- **Be flexible:** Things don't always go according to plan, so it's important to be flexible with your budget. If you spend more on one thing, cut back on something else.

Money Saving Tips

Here are a few money saving tips for your Barbados vacation:

1. Travel during the off-season. Accommodation and flights are typically cheaper during the off-season, which runs from June to November.

2. Stay in a self-catering apartment or villa. This will allow you to cook your own meals and save money on dining out.

3. Take public transportation. The buses and minibuses in Barbados are very affordable and efficient.

4. Eat at local restaurants. Restaurants in the local area are often more budget-friendly compared to dining establishments catering to tourists.

5. Take advantage of free activities. There are many free things to do in Barbados, such as swimming at the beach, hiking in the rainforest, and visiting the botanical gardens.

6. Buy a Barbados Bus Pass. If you plan on using the bus frequently, you can save money by buying a bus pass. Bus passes are available for one day, seven days, or one month.

7. Negotiate with taxi drivers. Taxi drivers in Barbados are willing to negotiate on the fare. Always make sure to discuss and agree upon the fare with the taxi driver before entering the vehicle.

8. Eat at Oistins Fish Fry. Oistins Fish Fry is a weekly event where you can enjoy fresh seafood and live music at affordable prices.

9. Take advantage of happy hour. Many restaurants in Barbados offer happy hour specials on drinks and food.

10. Visit Barbados during the Crop Over Festival. Crop Over is a two-month festival that celebrates Barbadian culture and heritage. There are many free events during Crop Over, such as street parades and concerts.

Useful Apps and Websites

Here are some useful apps and websites for a seamless Barbados vacation:

Apps

1. Barbados Tourism Authority App: This app provides a wealth of information on Barbados, including things to do, places to eat, and accommodation options.

It also includes a map of the island and a schedule of upcoming events. It also has a website

2. Barbados Bus: This app provides real-time bus arrival information. It also includes a route planner and a map of the bus network.

3. Barbados Weather: This app provides up-to-date weather information for Barbados. It also includes a forecast for the next seven days.

4. Barbados Restaurant Guide: This app provides a comprehensive guide to restaurants in Barbados. It includes reviews, menus, and contact information. It also has a website.

5. Barbados Attractions Guide: This app provides a guide to attractions in Barbados. It includes reviews, opening hours, and admission fees.

6. Currency Exchange Apps (e.g., XE, Currency Converter Plus): Having a currency exchange app on hand ensures you're always aware of the current exchange rates, helping you make informed financial decisions.

7. HappyCow: For vegetarians and vegans, HappyCow is a fantastic resource for finding plant-based dining options in Barbados.

Websites

1. Visit Barbados: This website is another great resource for information on Barbados. It includes a travel guide, blog posts, and a photo gallery. https://www.visitbarbados.org/

2. Barbados Property List: This website is a great resource for finding accommodation in Barbados. It includes a variety of options, from self-catering apartments to luxury villas.

3. Barbados.org: An independent website with information on all aspects of Barbados, including travel, accommodation, food, and activities.

Suggested Itineraries

Here is a comprehensive itinerary for a romantic long weekend getaway for two in Barbados:

Day 1

● Arrive at Grantley Adams International Airport (BGI) and check into your hotel.

● Head to the beach for a relaxing afternoon in the sun and sand. Some popular beaches include Carlisle Bay, Accra Beach, and Dover Beach.

● Have dinner at one of Barbados' many romantic restaurants. Some popular options include The Cliff, The Fish Pot, and Cin Cin by the Sea.

Day 2

● Visit Harrison's Cave, a stunning underground cave system with waterfalls and crystal-clear pools.

● Take a catamaran cruise to swim in the Caribbean Sea and snorkel with sea turtles.

- Have dinner at one of Barbados' many beachfront restaurants. Some popular options include The Sandpiper, The Lone Star, and Champers.

Day 3

- Visit Andromeda Botanic Gardens, a beautiful botanical garden with a variety of tropical plants and flowers.
- Have a couples massage at one of Barbados' many spas. Some popular options include the spa at Sandy Lane, the spa at The Crane Resort, and the spa at Fairmont Royal Pavilion.
- Have a romantic dinner at one of Barbados' many fine dining restaurants. Some popular options include The Tides, Daphne's, and The Fishy Pig.

Day 4

Have breakfast at your hotel and check out.

- Visit Oistins Fish Fry, a weekly event where you can enjoy fresh seafood and live music.
- Do some souvenir shopping at one of Barbados' many duty-free shops.

• Head to the airport for your flight home.

7-Day Family-Friendly Barbados Vacation Itinerary Creating Lasting Memories with Your Loved Ones

Day 1

• Morning: After arriving in Barbados and settling into your accommodation the previous day, head to a nearby beach like Accra Beach or Rockley Beach for a relaxing afternoon in the sun.

• Afternoon: Enjoy a casual beachfront lunch at a local eatery.

• Evening: Explore the lively atmosphere of St. Lawrence Gap, known for its restaurants, shops, and entertainment options.

Day 2

• Morning: Embark on an Island Safari tour for an off-road adventure through Barbados' natural beauty.

  - Explore the rugged interior, scenic viewpoints, and learn about the island's history and wildlife.

- Afternoon: Return to your accommodation for a leisurely afternoon by the pool or beach.
- Evening: Dine at a local restaurant to savor authentic Bajan cuisine.

Day 3
- Morning: Visit the Barbados Wildlife Reserve to see local and exotic wildlife in a natural setting.
- Afternoon: Head to Bathsheba Beach on the east coast to explore the unique rock formations and enjoy the picturesque scenery.
- Evening: Have a casual family dinner at a beachfront restaurant in Bathsheba.

Day 4:
- Morning: Explore Bridgetown's historic sites, including Independence Square, St. Michael's Cathedral, and the Barbados Museum.
- Afternoon: Visit George Washington House, where the first U.S. President stayed during his visit to Barbados.

• Evening: Enjoy a relaxed evening at your accommodation, perhaps with a family game or movie night.

Day 5

• **Morning:** Spend the morning at Crane Beach, known for its stunning pink sand and turquoise waters. Take part in optional water sports activities.

• Afternoon: Visit Oistins Fish Market for a casual lunch and experience the lively atmosphere.

• Evening: If visiting on a Friday night, enjoy the Oistins Fish Fry for delicious seafood and local entertainment.

Day 6

• Morning: Explore the fascinating underground world of Harrison's Cave with a guided tour.

• Afternoon: Head to the northern tip of the island to visit the Animal Flower Cave. Take in the breathtaking coastal views.

• Evening: Return to your accommodation for a relaxed evening.

Day 7

• Morning: Spend quality family time at a local amusement park or adventure activity center, like the Barbados Karting Experience or Aerial Trek Zipline Adventure.

• Afternoon: Enjoy a leisurely lunch at a nearby restaurant.

• Evening: Pack up and prepare for departure, cherishing the wonderful memories created during your Barbados vacation.

14-Day Solo Adventure, Unveiling the Wonders of Barbados

Day 1

• Morning: Arrive in Bridgetown, check in to your accommodation, and get settled.

• Afternoon: Explore Bridgetown's historic sites like Parliament Buildings and Independence Square.

• Evening: Enjoy a Bajan dinner at a local eatery.

Day 2

- Morning: Visit the Barbados Museum & Historical Society.
- Afternoon: Relax on Carlisle Bay Beach, try snorkeling, or take a boat tour.
- Evening: Savor a seafood dinner along the bay.

Day 3

- Morning: Head to Oistins Fish Fry for a taste of local culture and fresh seafood.
- Afternoon: Explore St. Lawrence Gap for shops, restaurants, and nightlife.
- Evening: Enjoy live music and dance at a local bar.

Day 4

- Morning: Explore Speightstown for its charming streets and art galleries.
- Afternoon: Visit Animal Flower Cave for breathtaking views and natural wonders.
- Evening: Dine at a seaside restaurant in the area.

Day 5

- Morning: Drive to the rugged north coast, stopping at Cherry Tree Hill and St. Nicholas Abbey.
- Afternoon: Visit Bathsheba for stunning vistas and surfing spots.
- Evening: Enjoy a sunset picnic at North Point.

Day 6:

- Morning: Discover the enchanting Hunte's Gardens.
- Afternoon: Explore Welchman Hall Gully and its unique plant life.
- Evening: Relax with a leisurely dinner at a nearby restaurant.

Day 7

- Morning: Explore the underground marvel of Harrison's Cave.
- Afternoon: Immerse yourself in the botanical wonders of Flower Forest.
- Evening: Indulge in a spa treatment or enjoy a quiet evening at your accommodation.

Day 8

- Morning: Head to Oistins Bay for a swim and relax on the beach.
- Afternoon: Visit the Barbados Wildlife Reserve for a taste of local fauna.
- Evening: Experience the vibrant nightlife in St. Lawrence Gap.

Day 9

- Morning: Spend more time at the Barbados Wildlife Reserve.
- Afternoon: Explore Farley Hill National Park for its lush landscapes and ruins.
- Evening: Enjoy a peaceful dinner back in Bridgetown.

Day 10

- Morning: Discover local crafts and art at Pelican Village.
- Afternoon: Stroll along the Bridgetown Boardwalk for scenic views.
- Evening: Dine at a waterfront restaurant in Bridgetown.

Day 11

- Morning: Travel to Bottom Bay for a relaxing day on the beach.
- Afternoon: Enjoy the tranquil surroundings and take in the stunning scenery.
- Evening: Return to your accommodation for a quiet night.

- **Day 12:**
- Morning: Head to Bathsheba's Soup Bowl for some surfing or beachcombing.
- Afternoon: Visit the historic St. John's Parish Church for its architecture and panoramic views.
- Evening: Dine at a local Bajan restaurant.

Day 13

- Morning: Take a tour of a local rum distillery to learn about Barbados' rich rum-making heritage.
- Afternoon: Relax or do some last-minute shopping in Bridgetown.
- Evening: Enjoy a farewell dinner at a fine dining restaurant.

Day 14

- Morning: Depending on your flight time, take a final stroll on the beach or do some last-minute shopping.
- Afternoon: Check out of your accommodation and head to the airport for your departure.

Travel Itinerary Planner

CONCLUSION

As you reach the final pages of this travel guide, I hope you're filled with anticipation and excitement for the adventure that awaits you in Barbados. The island's beauty, both in its landscapes and its people, is something truly special.

I want to take a moment to express my heartfelt gratitude for allowing me to be a part of your journey. It's been a pleasure guiding you through the wonders of Barbados, from the bustling streets of Bridgetown to the tranquil beaches of Bottom Bay.

I'd also like to extend a warm acknowledgment to the people of Barbados, whose hospitality and kindness make this island shine. Their smiles, their stories, and their warm welcomes are what make Barbados a place you'll carry in your heart forever.

As you embark on your Barbados adventure, may you find moments of joy, serenity, and wander around every corner. Cherish the memories you make, and know that the spirit of this island will stay with you long after you've returned home.

Safe travels, dear reader. May your journey be filled with new discoveries, meaningful connections, and the kind of happiness that only travel can bring. Until we meet again, whether in the pages of another guide or on a new adventure, may your heart always have a piece of Barbados.

Travel Itinerary Planner

Travel Itinerary Planner

Travel Itinerary Planner

Printed in Great Britain
by Amazon